SKILLS FOR SUCCESS

LEADERSHIP:
The Key to Management Success
by L. Bittel

MANAGING YOURSELF:
How to Control Emotion, Stress, and Time
by A. Goodloe, J. Bensahel, and J. Kelly

COMMUNICATING:
How to Organize Meetings and Presentations
by J. Callanan

HIRING THE RIGHT PERSON FOR THE RIGHT JOB
by C. Dobrish, R. Wolff, And B. Zevnik

MORALE AND MOTIVATION:
How to Measure Morale and Increase Productivity
by E. Benge and J. Hickey

ALFRED GOODLOE
JANE BENSAHEL
JOHN KELLY

MANAGING YOURSELF

HOW TO CONTROL EMOTION, STRESS, AND TIME

A GROLIER COMPANY

FRANKLIN WATTS

New York   London   Toronto   Sydney

Library of Congress Cataloging in Pubication Data

Goodloe, Alfred.
    Managing yourself.

    Includes index.
    1. Executives—Psychology. 2. Job stress—Prevention.
3. Executives—Time management. 4. Self-control.
I. Bensahel, Jane. II. Kelly, John. III. Title.
HF5500.2.G66   1984   658.4'095   84-7545
ISBN 0-531-09578-9

CONTENTS

PART II
CONTROLLING STRESS

PART III
CONTROLLING TIME

EXHIBITS

INTRODUCTION

The busy manager's day is taken up by all sorts of events: meetings to run to, telephones to answer, deadlines to meet, projects to complete, performance appraisals to conduct, bosses to report to, and a general have-it-done-by-five-o'clock-today atmosphere.

As you can most certainly attest to, it's not an easy job. Just when you don't think you can take it anymore, just when you've had your fill of the corporate life-style for the day, just when you start thinking about that long overdue vacation—Boom!—an unexpected crisis pops up, and you instinctively shift yourself back into high gear.

It's easy to understand why a few of the better-prepared managers eventually make it to the top while the vast majority simply fade away into obscurity.

This book, as its title suggests, divides your daily routine into three distinctly fundamental but absolutely essential elements: emotions, stress, and time.

In a nutshell, if you want to be a manager who makes the grade, who's able to handle the pressure-cooker life-style of the business world, and who makes it on your own terms, then this book is required reading for you.

The sections focus in detail on how you can maintain control over your emotions, stress, and time. Keep this in mind: if you don't control them, they will most certainly control you.

There are no simple answers to be found here; the answer still lies in hard work and sweat. But after reading this book and going through the various self-tests, checklists, charts, and quizzes, at least you'll know that you're aiming every bit of your time and energy in the right direction—toward your goal of reaching the top.

The first section deals with your emotions and the way in which you can use them to make yourself a better manager. The discerning manager knows that every decision, every communication, every effort, and every achievement contains an emotional element. People work in a climate dominated by emotional factors. And to get ahead, the manager who knows how to recognize and make use of those emotions is the one who will succeed.

All you have to do is turn the page . . . and start on your way to a more enjoyable—and more productive—career.

PART I

CONTROLLING EMOTIONS

EMOTIONS
AS A POWER BASE FOR
TODAY'S MANAGER

Emotions have three main uses for the manager. First, they are energy regulators. They enable you automatically to summon energy to meet an irritating, unique, or stressful situation. Tapping your emotional powers means learning how to utilize that energy.

Second, emotions help you gain an awareness of the degree to which you value certain things. "How do you *feel* about this new plan?" is a common inquiry. Getting in closer touch with your emotions improves your judgment. It makes you more sensitive to your own reactions to events and situations.

Finally, emotions are important in interpersonal relations. You can persuade or pacify or stimulate others by using your emotional powers. Emotions can block communication and cooperation, or enhance them.

WHAT EMOTIONS ARE NOT

Emotions are *not* personality. Someone may be boisterous or reserved, aggressive or passive. These are character traits, not emotions. Emotions are temporary feelings experienced by everyone.

Emotions are *not* irrational. Rational conclusions are always based on total evidence. Feelings are part of this evidence. Emotions no more interfere with rational thinking than do facts. Sometimes facts are wrong or misinterpreted; the same holds true for emotions.

Emotions are *not* weaknesses. They do not indicate a lack of control. They are natural reactions to your environment.

In fact, cold, unemotional people often expend so much energy suppressing their emotions that they have little left for a powerful response to the world.

The Continuity of Emotions

You do not just occasionally experience emotions. They are always with you. They shape and color your actions and perceptions even when you are unaware of them. Do not fall into the habit of ignoring your emotions until they demand your attention during a crisis.

Strong emotions affect you for hours, and sometimes for days. Emotions such as anger not only affect your psychological life but can have serious consequences for your physical health as well.

Your emotional life is a continuum. Emotions are interrelated and overlapping. Anger can develop into fear. Guilt can lead to anxiety. Even opposites like joy and sadness can be closely linked.

Emotion and Cognition

There is a close relationship between what you think—your cognition—and how you feel—your emotions. Each influences the other.

Negative thoughts can cause depression; aggressive thoughts can engender anger. Likewise, joyful thoughts can build optimism; fearful ones can tear down self-esteem.

This cognitive aspect of emotion is an important principle, one that you must understand if you want to utilize your emotional powers. You must realize that your emotions are not isolated or beyond your reach; they can be directly influenced by your thoughts. Directed thinking is an important tool for tapping your emotions.

SURVEY YOUR OWN EMOTIONS

Use Exhibit 1 to help you judge the degree to which you are using your emotional powers. It will help you determine the emotions on which you most need to concentrate. Review Exhibit 1 later as a check on your progress in developing emotional facility.

EXHIBIT 1

A Self-Test to Determine Your Emotional Powers

Anger	Often	Some-times	Seldom	Never
I hide or suppress my annoyance with others.	( )	( )	( )	( )

Anger	**Often**	**Some-times**	**Seldom**	**Never**
After I become angry with someone, I regret it.	( )	( )	( )	( )
Other people can push me into anger; I can't help it.	( )	( )	( )	( )
I consider my anger to be a handicap, not an aid.	( )	( )	( )	( )
I encounter situations where anger seems to be the only response open to me.	( )	( )	( )	( )

Joy

	Often	Some-times	Seldom	Never
My job seems mundane and devoid of any pleasure.	( )	( )	( )	( )
Boredom is a problem for me.	( )	( )	( )	( )
I have trouble really becoming immersed in my work.	( )	( )	( )	( )
My job seems to present me with nothing new.	( )	( )	( )	( )
When I get excited about a project, I fail to exercise sufficient caution.	( )	( )	( )	( )

Fear	Often	Some-times	Seldom	Never
When I avoid certain situations—such as flying or being in large crowds—I feel more comfortable.	( )	( )	( )	( )
I prefer to ignore things that I'm afraid of.	( )	( )	( )	( )
When I start thinking about a danger, I cannot control my thoughts.	( )	( )	( )	( )
I feel that failure is to be avoided at all costs.	( )	( )	( )	( )
To stop worrying is a difficult task for me.	( )	( )	( )	( )

Trust				
I'm not sure my abilities are sufficient for my job.	( )	( )	( )	( )
When subordinates want to approach a task in a different way than I would handle it, I become suspicious.	( )	( )	( )	( )
I feel most people are interested exclusively in themselves.	( )	( )	( )	( )
I avoid bringing my subordinates into decision-making and planning.	( )	( )	( )	( )

Trust	Often	Some-times	Seldom	Never
I try to hide my real feelings from others.	( )	( )	( )	( )

Envy

	Often	Some-times	Seldom	Never
The success of others seems to threaten me.	( )	( )	( )	( )
When I accomplish something, I make a point of informing people.	( )	( )	( )	( )
Seeing someone else receive an honor that I could just as well have had annoys me.	( )	( )	( )	( )
I tolerate no mistakes among my subordinates.	( )	( )	( )	( )
I see competition, not teamwork, as the best motivator for my subordinates.	( )	( )	( )	( )

Guilt

	Often	Some-times	Seldom	Never
When I am accused of making a mistake that is not my fault, I react poorly.	( )	( )	( )	( )
I dwell on inadvertent errors and feel that I must atone for them.	( )	( )	( )	( )

Guilt	Often	Some-times	Seldom	Never
I sense that I've done something wrong, but I'm not sure what it is.	( )	( )	( )	( )
My ethical standards are not clear to me.	( )	( )	( )	( )
By exaggerating, I magnify small wrongs that I commit.	( )	( )	( )	( )

Anxiety

	Often	Some-times	Seldom	Never
I am bothered by a vague sense of impending trouble.	( )	( )	( )	( )
My long-range goals are not clear in my mind.	( )	( )	( )	( )
Pressure on me seems to come from all directions at once.	( )	( )	( )	( )
Approaching a new project or an unfamiliar matter makes me uneasy.	( )	( )	( )	( )

Depression

	Often	Some-times	Seldom	Never
I have trouble falling asleep or staying asleep.	( )	( )	( )	( )
I am not able to concentrate on my work.	( )	( )	( )	( )

Depression	Often	Some-times	Seldom	Never
I have a feeling that my life is not under my control.	( )	( )	( )	( )
I sense that many of my accomplishments are undeserved.	( )	( )	( )	( )
I use constant activity as a way of getting through despondent moods.	( )	( )	( )	( )

Scoring

Often **5**; Sometimes **3**; Seldom **1**; Never **0**.

A score of 15 or more for any section indicates an emotional area you should concentrate on. A score of 5 or less indicates an area in which you already have some facility. Use your scores for each section to determine the priority for developing each emotional power.

USING ANGER
AS AN EFFECTIVE TOOL
IN BUSINESS

HOW WOULD YOU HANDLE IT?

Consider each of the following situations. Place a check mark next to the action you think would be the best way to handle it. In the space provided, briefly explain the reasoning behind your choice. Compare your reactions to the answers at the end of this chapter after you finish reading.

1. One of your subordinates promised to have an important report completed by a certain date. As that date approached, you reminded her of her commitment and received her reassurances that the report would be ready on time. The deadline arrives. You need the report for a meeting the next morning, but you discover at the end of the day that your subordinate has gone home without giving you the report and without explanation. You will have to take the blame for her failure. What should you do?

___ a. Put the incident entirely out of your mind.

___ b. Write a short memo to the subordinate telling her exactly what you think of her failure. Then put it in your desk.

___ c. Call in a colleague and talk with him about your subordinate's mistake.

___ d. Criticize your secretary for not reminding you to inquire once more about the report.

_____

_____

_____

2. An important customer is in your office complaining about delays in shipment of his company's orders. He becomes enraged, pounds his fists on your desk, and demands: "Can you do something about this, or are you as incompetent as you seem to be?" Your reply:

___ a. Calmly explain that you are not responsible and are as upset about the delays as he is.

___ b. Answer his insults with insults of your own.

___ c. Tell him forcefully that you will not stand for insults; then explain the delays and how you are going to rectify them.

___ d. Smile and suggest that he take a few minutes to cool off so you can discuss the matter reasonably.

_____

_____

_____

STRESS-PRODUCED ANGER

No one is more subject to anger-producing stress than the manager. You are constantly under pressure. You must handle colleagues and customers who are themselves often tense. You must accomplish your goals in spite of obstacles. You must come to grips with uncertainty. Your time is at a premium. As a result, if you do not learn to channel your anger, you will become its victim.

Anger is a natural reaction of your body and mind to an irritating stimulus. Physically and emotionally, anger is a preparation for confrontation.

NEGATIVE RESULTS OF ANGER

Two common reactions to anger often occur. The manager either suppresses the feeling, denying that anger exists even though it's raging inside. Or the manager expresses anger in an uncontrolled burst of temper. Neither reaction is very productive.

The physical problems that result from suppressing anger include high blood pressure, ulcers, teeth-grinding, and migraines.

Suppressed anger can be transformed into damaging psychological symptoms as well, including neurosis and depression. Unexpressed anger lowers self-esteem. People who dwell on how they should have acted during a confrontation come to think of themselves as cowards.

Anger can also cause self-destructive behavior. Suppressed anger allows people to avoid the realities of interpersonal relations. It can produce long-standing animosity among colleagues, and can inhibit communication within an organization.

People who become angry quickly tend to act before they think. The results are a distorted viewpoint, poor judgment, frequent errors, and damaged relations. Uncontrolled anger alienates others. It makes them defensive and antagonistic. Though they may comply with current orders, they will harbor resentment, which can emerge in many ways.

Quick-tempered people may also feel guilty about their anger. If such individuals feel that they cannot control their actions, self-doubt will eventually sink in, and the negative feedback those persons receive will reinforce their anger even more.

USING ANGER CONSTRUCTIVELY

Anger is not necessarily a negative emotion. If you handle it properly, you can turn it to your advantage. "Anger is commonly thought of as something to be controlled," says Raymond Novaco, a psychologist at the University of California, Irvine. "However, the positive attributes of anger are often overlooked." One of its most constructive facets is energy.

Two factors interfere with the utilization of anger energy. The first is overreaction. Unchecked, your body pumps more adrenaline into your system than you can handle. You become flooded with anger. Your rational control is blocked. While you are infused with the maximum amount of energy, you are unable to utilize it for productive purposes.

The second factor is misdirected energy. For example, one of your subordinates regularly makes a certain kind of mistake on a sales report. You have told her that she should be careful.

One reaction to a recurrence of the mistake is to lecture the subordinate angrily about her carelessness. A better use of your energy would be to analyze the way the subordinate compiles the reports. Find out why she makes this error. Then alter the form of the report to prevent future errors. Examples:

- A manager at a New York financial consulting firm set aside an hour to meet with a client. The client failed to show up at the appointed time and didn't call to cancel the meeting. The manager was furious. Instead of wasting the hour being upset, or confronting the client angrily, she attacked a complex analysis that she had been avoiding. Her newly directed energy allowed her to complete quickly what would otherwise have been a tedious task.

- The purchasing manager for an electronics company became angry with a supplier who was overcharging for a particular component. Rather than argue with the supplier, the manager used his anger to spur him to discuss substitute components with his engineering department. His efforts resulted in savings for the company.

Anger as a Communications Tool

"Anger can serve an important expressive function," Raymond Novaco says. "A healthy relationship depends on the ability of the partners to express anger and give each other negative feedback."

A judicious display of anger tells another person that this matter is important to you. It lets your colleague know that you are unhappy with the way things are going. He or she is then more likely to approach the matter as seriously as you do. Your co-worker doesn't have to guess how you feel about it. Exhibit 2 gives rules for properly expressing your anger. Example:

- A marketing manager had politely told a colleague several times not to interrupt him when he was in conference with a client. The colleague again opened the manager's

EXHIBIT 2

Rules for Expressing Your Anger

- Keep your remarks focused on the action, not on the person; in other words, criticize performance but not intelligence.

- Don't dwell on the past; refer only to the situation at hand.

- Never make references to another person's family, race, religion, social class, appearance, or manner of speaking.

- Don't limit other people's anger. When you shout, others have a right to shout back. Mutual anger can clear the air. If you take the attitude that you can become angry but your subordinates cannot, they will resent your anger.

- Don't hold a grudge.

- If you express unjustified anger against a person in front of others, you must apologize in front of others.

- Make sure you are angry with the right person. Don't blame a subordinate for a mistake that a supervisor is responsible for.

- Always ask for an explanation before you become angry. For example, if you berate a subordinate for not turning in a report on time and then find that you yourself misplaced it, your anger will make you look foolish.

- Make it clear *why* you are angry. If a subordinate's procrastination has forced you to waste your time, make that known to him or her.

- Avoid making threats. You may have second thoughts after you cool off; you will then be forced to back down.

- If possible, give the person a way out. If a co-worker offers to rectify the situation or to apologize for an offense, don't continue your anger.

door during such a meeting. The manager angrily told the colleague not to interrupt him. Afterward, the colleague apologized. He told the manager that he hadn't realized how important the matter was to him. In addition, the client was favorably impressed by the importance the manager gave to the meeting, as indicated by the manager's anger.

Using Anger to Establish Your Own Priorities

Just as anger tells others that the matter is important to you, your initial angry reaction can inform you yourself that something is wrong. In order to use the techniques to tap anger, you must be able to recognize the signs of anger early and use them as signals to alert you. Use Exhibit 3 to help you identify your own anger symptoms.

"When I feel that tightness in my face and find myself raising my voice at my secretary, I know I'm getting angry," says one manager. "It's time to go for a walk and cool down." When you recognize your anger before it affects your judgment or your relations with others, then you are properly tapping the power of anger.

A vice-president of a real estate company says she pays close attention to her anger during negotiations. "Signs of anger are like a cue to me," she says. "If I find myself clenching my fists during the talks, it tells me I'm being pushed too far. I look at the deal more critically to find out what I don't like about it."

Using Anger to Control the Aggression of Others

A moderate display of anger on your part can serve to moderate another person's aggressiveness, whereas passiv-

EXHIBIT 3

Recognizing Your Anger Symptoms

The physical effects of anger result from the body preparing, by means of a surge of adrenaline, to use energy faster. This change in body chemistry affects each person differently. Most people have one or two specific symptoms that indicate the beginning of anger. Check the symptoms that indicate anger in you.

_____tightening of muscles   _____cursing

_____speaking in a loud   _____a nervous tic
       voice

_____violent thoughts   _____flushing of the skin

_____a knot in the stomach   _____headache, pressure in
                                            the head

_____insomnia   _____quick, shallow
                                            breathing

_____distorted thinking   _____feeling light-headed

_____clenching the jaw   _____heat or chills

_____increased heart rate   _____making a fist

_____physically abusing an   _____slamming a door
       inanimate object, such
       as a pillow, desk, or   _____grabbing someone's
       pencil   arm

ity often exacerbates it. Researchers at Duke University placed students in a situation in which they thought they were giving electrical shocks to "opponents." When the "opponent" remained passive and pretended to suffer in silence, the students increased the level of shocks. When the "opponent" angrily protested, the students lessened the "punishment."

A sales manager at a securities company was having trouble with a supervisor who had a bad temper. When the supervisor entered the sales manager's office, he would angrily complain to her about some matter. The sales manager tried to calm him down and make him look at the matter rationally.

The supervisor's fits of temper continued. Finally, the sales manager responded angrily. After facing this unexpected angry response, the supervisor held his temper in check more often.

KEEPING AN ANGER DIARY

An anger diary can help you learn to use anger constructively. It allows you to identify frequent provocations, uncover patterns in your anger, and identify alternative ways of handling irritation.

Use a notebook for your diary entries. Make your notations as soon after each anger-producing incident as possible. Review the diary each week to keep track of the success of your anger-utilization efforts.

Each entry should include five parts.

1. a brief explanation of the incident that led to your anger

2. a rating of the degree of your anger on a scale from 1 (mildly irritating, no overt reaction) to 10 (infuriating)

3. the incidents, words, or actions (cues) that actually touched off your anger—a person's tone of voice, for example, or a particular remark

4. any underlying reasons for your anger—you felt upset about another matter; you were extrememly tired; you felt threatened

5. at least one constructive use of, or alternative to, anger in this situation

Example:

Incident	A man pushed ahead of me into a crowded elevator, and I had to wait for the next car.
Rating	4 (annoyed for ten minutes).
Cues	I was late for a meeting; the man who pushed me offered no apology.
Underlying cause	He failed to recognize the importance of my position in this company.
Alternatives	Reminding myself that it's only a short wait for me or that it will give me time to collect my thoughts for my meeting.

AN ANGER-UTILIZATION PROGRAM

As a manager, you face provocative situations every day. Two traditional pieces of advice for dealing with anger are "Don't take it personally" and "Wait until your emotions cool before you act."

Yet in many cases, you *are* personally involved in the situation and you *cannot* withdraw without appearing unassertive.

Professor Novaco describes a program for utilizing anger in his book *Anger Control* (Lexington, Mass.: Heath, 1975). He designed the program for those who must face provocation daily: managers, police officers, supervisors, and so forth. This system is based on six aspects of human anger. It draws on the positive, constructive aspects of this emotion.

Awareness. When was the last time you were angry? Some managers actually have to think back months. They do not recognize the minor feelings of anger that they quickly suppress. The earlier you recognize your anger, the more easily you can manage it, channel it productively, and keep it from escalating.

To improve your anger awareness, become sensitive to the patterns of your anger. If you keep an anger diary, regularly review your entries to discover the nature of your most common annoyances.

Ask questions such as these:

* Where do I most often become angry?

  ___ at home   ___ at outside meetings
  ___ in the office   ___ while traveling

* When does most of my anger occur?

  ___ early in the morning   ___ late in the afternoon
  ___ before lunch   ___ right after work

* With whom am I most frequently angry?

  ___ myself   ___ my secretary
  ___ a particular colleague   ___ strangers
  ___ my subordinates   ___ relatives

- What conditions contribute to my anger?

__ tiredness	____ prolonged loud noises
__ long hours at work	____ minor illness such as a cold
__ hunger	____ tension

Anger awareness also helps you keep your feelings focused. Consider, for instance, the manager of a consumer products company who received a marketing report each morning. He was very displeased with the marketing department and the reported results, but he was not aware that it was these reports that irritated him at the start of his daily routine. He let his angry feelings emerge by assuming a curt attitude toward his own subordinates. Increased anger awareness could have helped him prevent this inappropriate expression of his anger.

Self-esteem.   Threats to your sense of self-worth are an important anger-producing stimulus. Low self-esteem can make you susceptible to anger, while outside attacks can result in defensive anger. At the first sign of such anger, Professor Novaco recommends reinforcing your self-esteem by means of statements such as these:

- "I can handle this easily."

- "This is no reflection on my abilities."

- "This criticism is not justified."

Another way to use self-esteem to negate your anger is to block your internal critic. Don't let an error produce anger and lead you into further mistakes. Just correct yourself and go on to the next problem.

Suppose that your colleagues criticize you for making

a single mistake in the latest sales campaign, but they fail to acknowledge your considerable achievements. Instead of agreeing with their assessment and uselessly becoming angry over your perceived failure, remind yourself and them of the important contributions you have made.

Task orientation.   Once you recognize your anger, turn your attention to this question: What do I want to accomplish in this situation?

Task orientation does not mean suppressing your anger. A heated but controlled exchange with a colleague may serve an expressive purpose. Or anger may energize your efforts to rectify the situation. Let's say, for example, that a subordinate was supposed to compile sales figures for this month by noon today. He returns after a long lunch and still hasn't finished the job. A manager with an ego orientation might angrily shout, "You told me you'd have that done. Do you think you can get away with lying to me?" Taking a task orientation in the same situation, the manager might say, "Your delay is going to hold up everyone in this department. Perhaps you weren't aware of that. Next time, have more consideration for the rest of us." Appealing to the subordinate to show consideration for his colleagues puts pressure on him to work more efficiently. The manager's controlled anger tells him this is an important matter. Task orientation thus accomplishes goals rather than allowing anger to dissipate uselessly.

Skills.   Anger is partly habit. The person who frequently exhibits anger knows no other way to handle provocation. By learning other methods for dealing with anger-producing situations, such as compromise or reasoned discussion, you are less likely to exhibit unproductive anger.

A line manager at a large textile company was frequently

annoyed by her shipping supervisor. She engaged in heated arguments with the man about the late shipment of customers' orders. The shipping manager contended that it took a certain amount of time to process orders and that he couldn't speed up the process.

Since the manager's anger did little good, she tried a different technique. She sent the shipping supervisor photocopies of every irate letter she received from customers. Faced with evidence of the effects of his delay, the supervisor researched the shipping process and discovered new ways to speed delivery times.

To deal with provocative situations you can compromise and look for common ground. Use mediation and appeal to an authority on the matter. Express empathy by looking at the situation from the other person's point of view. Exhibit 4 reveals an assortment of other techniques for getting positive results in anger situations.

Reinforcement. Any technique that allows you to utilize your anger is reinforced when you use it successfully. Reward yourself with self-praise when you succeed in using your anger to your benefit. Tell yourself that it worked. You achieved what you wanted. That was easy. Your anger is less of a problem now. Your anger diary will help you to identify techniques that work for you. Learn to recognize when you use the technique. Congratulate yourself when you employ it successfully, and try to make a habit of it.

One manager became angry over the frequent mistakes of her younger subordinates. The technique she chose to utilize her anger was to imagine herself in her earlier days in her subordinates' situation. This allowed her to channel her anger into constructive advice. By reinforcing the technique each time she used it, she began to employ it as a matter of habit.

Relaxation. Tension is both an element and an instigator of anger. The ability to relax muscular tension quickly is a useful skill for preventing anger from building and for defusing anger during provocation. Everyone has his or her own special way to relax. You may take a coffee break, go for a walk, or simply recall a recent joyous occasion.

THREE TYPES OF ANGER

Anger takes three forms: *subjective anger* occurs when you become angry with yourself; *objective anger* reflects your anger at a situation or a group of people with whom you have no direct contact; and *interpersonal anger* happens when you are angry with a specific person and the possibility of direct confrontation exists.

Though everyone experiences all three types of anger, most managers find that they have particular difficulty with one variety. This is largely a result of personality. If you are an introverted person for example, you might become angry at yourself in a situation in which an extrovert would blame someone else.

One of the keys to tapping the emotional power of your anger is to identify the variety that most commonly affects you. Exhibit 4 is designed to help you do just that. After rating yourself, you can discover where you should concentrate your efforts. Use the following information to enhance those efforts.

Addressing Subjective Anger

The first step in tapping subjective anger is to avoid blaming yourself. Anyone would be annoyed, for example, by hav-

EXHIBIT 4

Creating Your Own Anger Profile

Here are some examples of the three types of anger. Imagine each act happening to you. Then rate the degree of anger you would be likely to feel. Use a scale from 1 to 10 as you did in your anger diary (1, no reaction; 10, infuriating).

Add up your score for the seven items in each section. If you score over 50 in any section, you are particularly susceptible to that type of anger. If you score less than 25, this kind of anger is not much of a problem for you.

Subjective Anger

_____You make an easily avoidable mistake while working with figures.

_____You misplace something and have to spend ten minutes searching for it.

_____You rush to a meeting and fail to bring the necessary materials.

_____You put a letter in your pocket but forget to mail it.

_____Your competitor uses a marketing technique that you should have thought of first.

_____You take a client to dinner, but leave your credit card at home.

_____In an argument with a colleague, you feel you have not been assertive enough.

SCORE: _____

Objective Anger

_____Monetary inflation continues to soar.

_____Your sales department fails to meet its quota for the second month in a row.

_____Government rules increase your company's paperwork.

_____A crucial machine in your plant breaks down.

_____One of your customers goes out of business without paying his debts.

_____You hear of a serious and senseless crime in your neighborhood.

_____You regularly work overtime while some colleagues go home early.

SCORE: _____

Interpersonal Anger

_____A colleague complains loudly about a small oversight you made.

_____You are discussing a problem with a subordinate when an unwelcome third party intervenes.

_____You are blamed for a mistake made by another.

_____You telephone someone and that person fails to return your call.

_____Someone is unnecessarily rude to you.

_____A person interrupts while you are trying to concentrate.

_____A waiter gives you and a client poor service in an expensive restaurant.

SCORE: _____

ing to waste time looking for a misplaced object. But never direct your anger at yourself.

Second, stay objective about the consequences. You forget to mail a letter. Is there really any rush? You fail to bring a folder to a meeting. Is it very inconvenient to go back for it? Keep each incident in perspective.

Third, channel your anger into productivity. If you are mad at yourself for misplacing a letter, use that energy to revamp your filing system. If you feel that you are not assertive enough and if that makes you angry with yourself, participate in an assertiveness training seminar. If you make mistakes, use the energy to double-check your work, not to worry about your errors.

Finally, remember that becoming angry at yourself is often a symptom of another problem—overwork, tension, or fatigue, perhaps. Use the anger as a warning. Probe for a deeper problem and address it.

Channeling Objective Anger

The key to tapping objective anger is to ask, "What can I do about this problem?" Take the example of the manager who drives to the office and is frequently held up in traffic. At first, the delays made him furious, agitated, and tense. Then he asked, "What can I do about this situation?"

He purchased a portable dictation machine so that he could dictate letters and memos while he was stuck in traffic jams. The delays still annoy him. But he directs his anger energy into his work instead of wasting it.

This strategy works well with any objective anger. If you're angry about the increasing rate of inflation, for example, you can form or join a business council to study ways to fight it. If you are annoyed by your sales department's mediocre efforts, you can channel your anger into giving the sales force a pep talk or creating a new sales program. If your heavy work load makes you angry, you can use that anger to develop a plan for delegating the work more efficiently.

Difficulties with Interpersonal Anger

Interpersonal anger is the most difficult form to tap because the presence of another person adds an unpredictable element to the situation. When, for example, the other person is eager for a confrontation, it is difficult to turn his or her anger into productive channels. However, you can use interpersonal anger for a number of useful purposes:

To break down barriers.   Two colleagues have worked closely together and developed mutual respect. While attacking a difficult problem, one feels that the approach of the other is wrong. She makes a polite suggestion. The other disregards it. The problem continues. Eventually the first manager becomes angry. She engages in a heated discussion about the matter with her colleague. The latter finally listens, and the two of them communicate. Anger has provided the forcefulness to break through the barrier of professional reserve.

To teach.   A production manager arranged to meet a subordinate in the company's lumber mill to examine some machinery. The subordinate appeared without a hard hat, in violation of company policy. The manager shouted at him in angry and forceful tones, "Don't ever forget the safety rule again." He never did. Anger has the power to impress on others the vital importance of the point you are making.

To stimulate. A purchasing manager assigned a subordinate to negotiate with a supplier. The subordinate came back with the supplier's best offer. His boss, angered by the report, demanded that he get a better price. His superior's anger energized the complacent subordinate. He went to the supplier determined to work out a better deal, and did so.

In all demonstrations of interpersonal anger, act judiciously. Anger can create barriers as well as break them down, can produce dismay as well as teach, and can discourage as well as stimulate. Keep your anger within bounds.

HANDLING ANGER IN OTHERS

The key to success in handling anger in others is to recognize its causes. A manager at an insurance company required her secretary to type a long actuarial report each week. The manager found that, though her secretary was an excellent typist, she frequently made mistakes on this document. The manager finally confronted her secretary with this problem. The secretary told her that, when she worked with the manager's colleague, she had never been required to type these reports. She was angry about the extra work. Her resentment showed in the poor job she did in typing them. After a frank discussion and adjustments in her work load, the secretary began to turn in her usual carefully typed reports.

Be alert for signs of unexpressed anger: someone may become unusually quiet, the pitch or tone of that person's voice may lower, or a nervous habit may appear, like clicking a ballpoint pen.

Let the person know that you are sympathetic: "I realize this situation irritates you." Try to get the individual to talk about his or her feelings: "What do you think? Is this a problem for you?" Don't let anger build into long-term resentment. Help make the person's anger productive.

In dealing with people who are easily angered:

- Keep your own anger under control. Avoid a shouting match.

- Don't remain detached. A common way to irritate angry people even further is to act as if the matter is of little importance to you. Let them know you are concerned. Listen carefully to what they are saying. Raise your own voice if necessary.

- Allow others to express their anger. Unless they are violent, it is better to hear them out than to say, "Go relax."

- Empathize. Why are they angry? Do they feel threatened? Are they projecting malicious motives onto you?

- Sympathize. Tell them you understand that they feel strongly about this matter, that anyone would be upset by it.

- Work for a resolution. "What are we going to do about this? What do you suggest?" Let them know they are having an influence on how the matter is worked out.

When you deal with subordinates or colleagues who have frequent angry outbursts rather than occasional ones, invite them to have a private talk with you about their anger. Point out how their angry outbursts interfere with their productivity and that of the company. Let them know that you are interested in helping them channel their anger to improve, not hinder, their effectiveness.

Encourage people to talk about their anger. How do they feel about it? What things irritate them? Suggest they apply the principles of anger management such as task orientation, an anger diary, recognition and analysis of provocative situations, and positive self-statements.

ANSWERS:
HOW WOULD YOU HANDLE IT?

1. The best choice is *b*. Write the memo and put it in your desk. This will take the weight of anger off your mind and help you relax. Putting your exact thoughts on paper will also help you to avoid exaggeration. You can decide what to do about the subordinate's lapse the next day when you confront her. Trying to forget an incident rarely works when you are upset. Criticizing the subordinate to a colleague gives expression to your anger, but may be an action you later regret. Diverting your anger by putting the blame on your secretary is unfair and accomplishes nothing.

2. The most effective solution is *c*. Standing up for yourself indicates to the customer that you take the matter as seriously as he does, but you prefer not to discuss it on a personal level. It also reinforces your self-respect. Your explanation then serves to calm his rage and return the discussion to a rational level. Calmly telling him to cool off, or expressing concern without showing it will only serve to increase his anger. Trading insults makes you both less reasonable and does not move you toward a solution to the problem.

3

THE IMPORTANCE
OF FINDING JOY IN YOUR WORK

HOW WOULD YOU HANDLE IT?

Consider each of the following situations. Place a check mark next to the action you think would be the best way to handle it. In the space provided, briefly explain the reasoning behind your choice. Compare your reactions to the answers at the end of this chapter after you finish reading.

1. You have mastered your responsibilities and effectively manage your subordinates. Your department operates smoothly. In spite of this, you feel uninspired. You no longer find pleasure in your work. Your daily routine sometimes seems tedious. You have trouble maintaining interest in your activities. What is the best means of restoring joy to your work life?

___ a. Take a long vacation and get a change of scenery.

___ b. Acquire new hobbies and outside interests.

— c.   Restructure your job so that you have to learn new skills.

— d.   Become more involved in the details of your job.

— e.   Do nothing and wait for the boredom to pass.

_____

_____

_____

2.   One of your subordinates takes a great deal of interest in his work. When involved with a new project, he often becomes so enthusiastic that he exaggerates its potential benefits. He spends more time on his favorite tasks than they warrant. Confronted with tough obstacles, however, he loses interest quickly. How can you make him more effective?

— a.   Include him only in the planning stages of a project.

— b.   Take away his authority and assign him to routine tasks.

— c.   Make him a member of a committee or task force.

— d.   Be more critical of his mistakes.

— e.   Shift him frequently from one project to another.

_____

_____

_____

PROFESSIONAL BENEFITS OF JOY

Joy is an emotion that arises from the release of internal tension or conflict. The psychic energy that has been tied up in tension flows into you. You suddenly feel fresh, and you experience a surge of strength. You have experienced this *restorative effect* yourself. At work on a difficult business problem, for example, you seem to be getting nowhere. The work seems tedious and endless. Suddenly a new idea occurs to you. You see an opening, a possible solution. The joy of discovery revives you. You are no longer fatigued but attack the problem with new enthusiasm and energy.

Enthusiastic, energized managers *inspire* their colleagues and subordinates to make new and more confident efforts to overcome problems. In contrast, managers who lack joy in their work do not inspire. Their subordinates often reflect their lethargy. Managers who are open to joy benefit not only themselves but their entire organization. They are easier to communicate with and form deeper bonds with their co-workers, promoting *teamwork*.

Besides giving you energy, joy helps you overcome frustration. It gives you a clear signal that you are on the right track. Joy wipes away doubts. It strengthens both *confidence* and the courage to persevere. Tension and stress are a part of every manager's life. When you experience joy, you unlock many tensions inside you. You relax.

IDENTIFYING THE SOURCES OF JOY

If your business life, like that of many managers, seems lacking in joy and enthusiasm, look into the following sources from which joy can emerge. Your goal is to open yourself to joy, to accept it, not to force it.

Activity. The busy manager is less likely to feel dull than the one who has excess time. Engaging in plenty of hard, results-oriented work is the first rule for achieving joy.

Sharing.   Sharing and generosity naturally give rise to joy. Not only is enthusiasm contagious for other members of a group, but sharing it helps to sustain it in yourself. The best way to build enthusiasm for a project or idea is to talk about it with your colleagues.

Teamwork.   Teamwork is a source of joy. A task force of people with diverse talents working together to solve a problem often yields more satisfaction to each member than a single manager achieves by addressing the problem alone.

Immersion.   For many managers, the joy of total immersion in a task is an infrequent event. They are plagued by interruptions and multiple tasks. You can increase the joy you find in your work by scheduling uninterrupted periods to devote to work that you find engrossing.

Physical pleasure.   Too often, in the rush of daily life, the pressured manager fails to savor the pleasures of hard exercise, food, or a pleasant view. To draw joy from the physical world, turn your attention away from the worries of business and focus it on your senses. Don't allow problems to suffocate your enjoyment of simple pleasures.

Discovery.   Habit and routine dull your sense of discovery. In order to regain this joy, break out of your patterns and learn new skills.

A personnel manager in an insurance company found that her job had become tedious. She wondered if some of the more laborious work couldn't be done on a computer. She began to study data processing in personnel administration and gradually became highly knowledgeable. She was able to increase her department's productivity, and she advised other sectors on the potentials of electronic data processing. She found that the problems she faced and the new knowledge she acquired were stimulating and enjoyable.

Achievement. As a manager, you must constantly attack the difficulties that lie before you. As a result, you may sometimes forget that you are regularly solving problems and achieving goals. Sit back and savor your achievements. Make a list of what you have accomplished in the past month. The difficult, boring, painstaking work that goes into a project actually adds to the joy of achievement. Don't always immediately leap forward to the next problem. Enjoy the outcome of a successful negotiation, the solution of a production problem, or the launching of a new product.

MAINTAINING EMOTIONAL BALANCE

While joy and enthusiasm can brighten your entire professional life, they can also get out of control. An overly enthusiastic manager can become gullible and inconsistent. Your goal is to tap the energy of joy while maintaining a balanced perspective. Be on the alert for the following symptoms of overenthusiasm in yourself and in your subordinates.

Distortion. Risks are not properly considered; values are not given their due. Enthusiastic responses replace rational evaluation.

Misplaced priorities. Even a usually sensible manager can become so involved in a favorite project that he or she neglects far more important work. Overenthusiasm can weaken the sense of proportion.

Exaggeration.   Overenthusiastic managers often expect a great deal more from a project they are excited about than it can produce. They exaggerate the positive and ignore the negative elements. They become gullible because they want to believe only good about the object of their enthusiasm. They may even deny obvious contradictory facts.

Inconsistency.   Managers with too much enthusiasm often give up too easily. Once they become disillusioned with a project they tend to drop it completely and turn their attention elsewhere. They don't push projects through to completion. They are impatient, looking for quick results.

Alienation.   Enthusiasm is contagious, arousing the interest and participation of others. Overenthusiasm often has the opposite effect. Sometimes, in a rush to accomplish a task, a manager becomes careless of the feelings and prerogatives of others, ignoring rules of courtesy and lines of authority and rejecting criticism.

FIVE QUESTIONS TO BALANCE YOUR ENTHUSIASM

When you are presented with an idea or project about which you are particularly enthusiastic, take the time to make sure you are not falling victim to overenthusiasm. Ask yourself these questions:

1. If all goes well, what is the best possible outcome that I can realistically expect from this project?

2. Every idea is subject to problems and obstacles. What are the main ones to expect here and how can I overcome them?

3. How do the probable benefits of this project compare with the payoffs on other tasks for which I am responsible?

4. All ventures entail risks. How do the risks involved in this particular project compare with the potential achievement?

5. What are the underlying assumptions and expectations that are responsible for my enthusiasm? Have I correctly evaluated them?

PRIDE AS A COMPONENT OF JOY

Two kinds of pride contribute to joy. The first is overall pride in yourself, your sense of self-worth. Self-respect and self-value are essential components of the capacity for pleasure. Such pride allows you to act with confidence and assurance. It gives you the capacity to appreciate the everyday achievements of your life, and it provides you with the courage to act boldly and decisively.

The second kind of pride is specific pride, often a direct component of joy. This involves the feeling of accomplishment you experience when you finish an important project or recognize your own achievements. It allows you to reward youself. You don't wait for outside recognition.

Exhibit 5 gives you some hints for boosting your pride and confidence.

EXHIBIT 5

Five Ways to Boost Your Pride and Self-Esteem

1. *Don't compare yourself with others.* While a certain amount of competitiveness is healthy, your abilities, opportunities, and achievements are your own. Give them the worth they are due. Don't exaggerate or diminish them by setting them against those of another.

2. *Reward yourself.* Reinforce your feelings of pride by rewarding yourself for a job well done. When you finish a demanding project or land a big account, go out for a meal at a good restaurant. Take a half-day off to enjoy yourself. Note your sense of accomplishment; then return to work refreshed.

3. *Accept praise.* Don't make the mistake of indulging in false modesty. If a colleague congratulates you for a new record in your department, don't say, "It was nothing." Thank your friend and enjoy the feeling of pride you experience.

4. *Accent the positive.* When talking with colleagues and friends, don't dwell on the mistakes you've made or the problems you face. Talk instead about your achievements and what they mean. Don't be afraid to say, "I'm proud of that."

5. *Avoid self-criticism.* Since you have the closest view of your own errors, weaknesses, and doubts, you may have a tendency to emphasize those and ignore your accomplishments, strengths, and talents. Don't become too self-critical. If you've tried hard, be proud of your efforts even if they haven't all succeeded.

ANSWERS: HOW WOULD YOU HANDLE IT?

1. The best solution is *c*. Some change is needed. But a vacation will tend to increase your dissatisfaction. Outside interests do nothing to address the real problem of finding joy in your work. More involvement in details of your present duties only deepens your monotony. Learning new skills and taking a different approach to your responsibilities will awaken the joy of discovery and achievement.

2. The best choice is *c*. Your goal is to tap his enthusiasm, not to dampen or neutralize it. Arranging for him to work in a group allows the other members to exert a modifying influence on his ardor without stifling him.

4

HOW TO
TURN FEAR INTO A
BUSINESS ALLY

Fear is a fundamental emotion, a basic tool of survival. It affects everyone. Your goal is not to be free of fear but to recognize it, to control it, and to turn it to your own advantage. Before considering how to deal with the fears that every manager faces, you should know something about fear in general. Test your knowledge about fear by answering the following questions True or False. Then read the answers following them for facts about fear.

TRUE-FALSE QUIZ:
FACTS ABOUT FEAR

___ 1. The symptoms of fear are much like the symptoms of anger.

___ 2. Fear can become a habit.

___ 3. Courage is the absence of fear.

___ 4. Stress increases resistance to fear.

___ 5. Chronic fear drains a person of energy.

___ 6. You must uncover the origin of fear in order to deal with it.

___ 7. The best way to deal with fear is to rationalize it.

___ 8. Fear of fear is only a figure of speech, not a genuine problem.

___ 9. Many people are afraid of speaking in public.

___ 10. Fear of success is not limited to lower-echelon managers.

Answers

1. True. Both fear and anger are mechanisms whose function is the quick use of energy by the body. The blood surges, heart pounds, the mouth becomes dry, the muscles tense. Both increase energy and alertness.

2. True. One of the problems in dealing with fear is that its habitual nature creates fear even in the absence of real danger.

3. False. "Courage is resistance to fear, mastery of fear— not absence of fear," said the American writer Mark Twain. The courageous person notes his or her fears and uses them rather than being mastered by them.

4. False. Stress and fatigue tend to make you more susceptible to unreasonable fears.

5. True. Chronically fearful or anxious people suffer from lack of energy. The reasons: intense or chronic fear

causes the muscles to release sugar into the blood, denying them the food for metabolism; and the mental effort awakened by fear uses up energy that would otherwise be available for productive work.

6. False. Psychologists today advise that you do not need to uncover the origins or underlying causes of your fears in order to bring them under control. Instead, you should focus on what sets off the fear and how you can use it. Many people do know the origin of their fears, but still allow those fears to affect them adversely.

7. False. "I'm right to be afraid to make this budget decision on my own. Look at the mistake I made the last time I did so." This kind of thinking reinforces unreasonable fears by making them appear rational. A more productive thought: "I have handled plenty of budget matters successfully in the past; one mistake doesn't mean much."

8. False. In the condition known as agoraphobia, a common and debilitating phobia, the person's main fear is of his or her own panic. In addition, because of the social stigma often connected with fear, many people are afraid to acknowledge and deal with their ordinary fears. Thus their fear of fear hampers them from effectively handling normal reactions.

9. True. Speaking in public is one of the most often cited fears, occurring in about 45 percent of adults. Surveys also show that as many as 40 percent of adults are afraid of heights.

10. True. You are most likely to suffer the fear of success when you are at or near the top of your profession.

IDENTIFYING YOUR FEARS

Facing your fears is the first step in bringing them under control and making them work for you. Because fear is an unpleasant emotion, most people tend to avoid fear-producing situations whenever possible. As a result, they often are not consciously aware that fear is affecting their lives. Even the thought of the feared object may arouse unpleasant symptoms, so the person doesn't think about the fear.

In order to uncover your own fears, consider whether you have ever experienced any fear of certain objects or situations. A number of items commonly invoke fear in many people. Most people fear a few specific places, actions, or objects. For example, you might be wary of making new product decisions or of confronting a certain person. List all your fears, no matter how minor. The next step is to determine the *cost* of your fear. A fear of snakes, for example, will have little effect on the life of a city dweller who never encounters them.

However, if a fear produces any of the following reactions, it has to be addressed.

Limitation.   Is a certain fear limiting the scope of your social or business life? Are you spending energy avoiding the feared object? Does your fear constrain other aspects of your activities?

Agitation.   While fears can be a way of dealing with stress, they can also become a source of constant tension. Do you fear something you cannot avoid? Do you experience active symptoms connected with this fear more than once a week.

Self-fulfillment. Fears can fulfill themselves. If you are afraid of failure, you may lower your ambition to such an extent that you do indeed fail. If you feel rejection, you may constrain your spontaneity to such an extent that you foster rejection. Is your fear contributing to the undesirable result rather than helping you to cope?

ANALYZING YOUR FEARS

After you have identified your fears and evaluated their cost, list the three or four principal fears that you want to deal with. Once you have brought these fears under control and turned them to your own benefit, return to your list of fears and address some others.

Fear analysis prepares you to deal with your fears. Particularly with minor fears, the analysis itself can help keep fears from having a negative impact on your life. Make copies of Exhibit 6 for as many of your current fears as you wish to analyze. Fill them in after reading the directions and studying the Example of Fear Analysis that follows.

Fear   Identify your fear as directed above.

Effects   List the cost of the fear, the specific effects it has on your life. Include the projected benefit of bringing the fear under control.

Cues   What are the situations or circumstances in which you experience the fear? Are these conditions present in your surroundings? Are you afraid when you're with specific people? Do thoughts of an object cause your fear? Do you feel the fear when you are alone? With others?

EXHIBIT 6

Fear Analysis Worksheet

Fear

Effects

Cues

Specific Fear

Worst Outcome

Realistic Evaluation

Specific Fear	Most general fears can be narrowed to specific ones. A person who is afraid of heights may actually fear being pushed from a high place. A fear of making mistakes may actually be a fear of being ridiculed by subordinates.
Worst Outcome	What is the absolute worst that can happen with regard to your fear? For example, if you are afraid of being criticized by a colleague,

your specific fear may be that you will become extremely angry with the person. The worst results: he criticizes you, you yell at him, you lose his friendship, he deliberately causes you severe job problems.

Realistic Evaluation

What is the likelihood that the worst outcome will occur? For instance, in the example above, if you are criticized, you will probably be able to control your anger; if you get angry, you'll keep your reaction within bounds; if you become violently angry, you probably will at least be able to make up for it later. Seen from this viewpoint, your fear seems exaggerated and unreasonable.

EXAMPLE OF FEAR ANALYSIS

Fear

Public speaking.

Effects

Nervousness interferes with my ability to give an effective speech. I avoid occasions on which it would be good for my career to give a talk. I don't pay attention in a large meeting because I am afraid of being called on to speak. Controlling fear would increase my self-confidence and concentration.

Cues

Having to speak before a group of five or more people whom I don't know; thinking of giving such a speech; being in a large meeting where I could be called on to talk.

Specific Fear

Appearing foolish and incompetent before a crowd.

Worst   I speak before a large group and I panic com-
Outcome   pletely so that I'm unable to continue. As a
            result, I'm widely ridiculed.

Realistic   Even in the worst instance I could probably
Evaluation refer to my notes and continue. If I did panic,
            I probably wouldn't be ridiculed, since many
            people share this fear.

FEAR AS A STIMULUS TO ACTION

Reasonable fear stimulates an individual to develop effective countermeasures. Fear of a business recession, for example, encourages formation of contingency plans. The key to using functional fear is to recognize and control its level. Moderate fear stimulates, while intense fear paralyzes.

A manager of a manufacturing firm was extremely fearful of the consequences of his being incapacitated even briefly. He didn't recognize the exact source of his uneasiness at first. He finally faced up to what was bothering him. None of his subordinates was prepared to take over his duties. He eventually acknowledged his fear as a reasonable one and immediately began to train an assistant to take over in his absence.

Fear can prompt you to be more thorough in preparing for a stressful event, helping to reduce the ill effects of the stress. An account executive may be fearful of her first meeting with an important prospective client. The fear, properly acknowledged, prompts her to go over possible questions and problems that may arise in the course of the interview.

One beneficial effect of fear is that it heightens vigilance. Studies have shown that a moderately fearful person is more alert in hearing and sight than a nonfearful one. For instance, fear of novelty—of entering a new market, of meeting new people, of traveling to a strange country—is a common and useful fear. If kept under control, it can help you learn about and evaluate a new experience quickly. Fear can also alert you to possible dangers in an unfamiliar situation. Since your business environment is always changing, a moderate fear of novelty can make you a more effective manager.

CONTROLLING FEAR THROUGH DESENSITIZATION

To use fear you must keep it at a moderate level. Some psychologists recommend that people take a behavioral approach to controlling fear. Rather than try to analyze the underlying basis of intense or irrational fears, you simply eliminate the fear-causing behavior. One way is through desensitization, which involves three steps:

1. *Relaxation.* You must develop the ability to relax deliberately. Controlling your breathing will aid you in relaxation.

2. *Fear hierarchy.* Think of a fear you want to learn to control. Imagine a number of situations in which you would experience the fear, ranging from minimally fear-producing to terror-inducing. Give each situation a rating from 0 to 100 according to the level of fear it produces. Think of scenes closer and closer to the worst one you can imagine as your rating goes up. For example, if you fear heights, list looking out a second-floor window, then peering down from a fifth-floor balcony. Finally, imagine looking down from a tenth-floor railing.

3. *Mastery*. Now combine relaxation with your fear hierarchy. You can do this either in reality—by actually putting yourself into the situations you have listed—or with imagery—by vividly imagining the scenes. Start with the least fear-provoking item. If it arouses any fear or tension, take time to relax. Then come back to it. Relax again. Keep repeating this exercise until you can encounter the item without fear. Only then should you proceed to the next item in your hierarchy. The point is not to generate fear each time. It is to experience progressively more intense stimuli *without* fear.

ADDITIONAL METHODS FOR CONTROLLING FEAR

Rational knowledge cannot eliminate all fears, but it is an aid in controlling fear. A large element of any fear is the unknown. Learn as much as possible about the object of your fear. Not only will you gain control over your fear, but you will also pick up useful information. For example, if you are afraid of a fire in your office building, learn about the fire safety system of the building. In this way, your fear will work for you, not against you.

Manuel Zane, a New York City psychotherapist, used this technique with a group of people who were intensely afraid of riding in elevators. He arranged for a representative of the Otis Elevator Company to give his patients a course in the workings of elevators. Over a ten-week period, they studied all the mechanisms and safety devices connected with elevator operation. After that period, all his patients were able to ride in elevators without experiencing noticeable fear.

Flooding, also known as implosion therapy, is the opposite of desensitization. It was developed by Thomas Stampfl of the University of Wisconsin. In flooding, you "stare down your nightmares" by putting yourself directly into a highly fear-producing situation, usually through imagery. Rather than avoid the fear, you experience it until you become immune to it.

It is important in flooding to prevent any punishment that would reinforce the fear. For example, if you are afraid of elevators, don't suddenly push your way into a crowded elevator. Instead, vividly imagine being trapped in a crowded elevator. Arouse your fear but not the punishment of the panic reaction. Flooding should be used for profound and deep-seated fears only with the guidance of a therapist. But it can also be useful for dealing with minor fears. It has the advantage of being the quickest way to bring the fear under control.

FEAR OF FAILURE

Fear of failure is common among managers. Because they have great responsibility, the consequences of their failures are profound. Furthermore, they are highly visible, so many people witness their failures. Also, they may develop the feeling that they can master almost any situation. As a result, failure has a deep impact on their self-image.

This fear can become one of your most useful emotions. It can temper your judgment, prompt you to give the necessary attention to detail, energize you to make that extra effort toward success, and generally motivate your entire approach to your job.

Unfortunately, the fear of failure can also be detrimental. It can paralyze you. You avoid taking any risks for fear of failing. You avoid responsibility. You keep yourself from learning new skills and engaging in new experiences because you are afraid of being unsuccessful. You lower your standards to make "success" easier.

Try the following four methods for keeping fear of failure under control so that it works for you, not against you:

1. *Limit your mental exposure.* Don't think that because you failed at one task, you'll fail at the next. Don't stake your entire self-worth on any one project or task. Even the worst failure leaves large areas of your business life in which you are successful. And no failure can wipe out the successes that brought you to your current position.

2. *Balance process and product.* Avoid evaluating your performance exclusively on the basis of outcome, disregarding your individual effort. In some situations, you are bound to fail no matter how hard and skillful your efforts; circumstances may be against you. But in the results-oriented world of business, many managers begin to judge themselves exclusively on what they produce, not on their sincere efforts. Take the attitude that success may mean trying as hard as possible, not just obtaining the desired result.

3. *Avoid perfectionism.* It is rare that anything works out as expected. Don't fall into the habit of labeling partial successes as failures.

4. *Value failure.* Failure can be the foundation of success. You will become less fearful of failure if you accept the fact that an occasional failure is a necessary component of achievement. There can be no growth or discovery without risk of failure. Consider how previous failures contributed to past successes.

FEAR OF SUCCESS

Fear of success is a paradox. Usually, people fear what is undesirable. Success is desirable. So why would men and women fear it? Yet they do. Consider young managers in their constant struggle to prove themselves, to work their way up in a corporate hierarchy. When they attain the positions they have striven for, they sometimes feel let down. Even some high-level managers fear that once they have reached the top, they will be more susceptible to falling backwards. They fear too much success.

While not a common emotion among managers, fear of success does exist. Here are some reasons:

- *Disappointment*. Having reached a high position, you realize that achievement is not all you imagined it to be. You find that long hours and tedious work are still required.

- *Ostracism*. Success may cut you off from the camaraderie you formerly experienced with your colleagues.

- *Conflicting aspirations*. You are a research scientist, and you receive the chance to become vice-president of research and development. But success in this direction would preclude your hope of making significant contributions in your scientific field.

- *Freedom and power*. As an executive, you may feel uncomfortable with the wide freedom and authority that success makes available to you.

- *Competition*. You may be fearful that your success will make you a target for colleagues who are envious of your status.

- *Conflicting demands.* You see that your success will limit the time you can spend with your family or on some favorite outside activity.

Evaluating Fear of Success

Some of the effects of the fear of success are similar to what some managers feel in the fear of failure. They don't want to take risks because they might succeed. They refuse to probe the limits of their abilities. They are overly humble, not taking proper credit for their achievements.

If you are suffering from this problem, ask yourself the following questions. In most instances, self-evaluation will neutralize the fear of success.

- What are my career goals?

- How have these goals changed over the years?

- Is the position I am striving for really the best one for me?

- Are there elements of my life that conflict with these goals?

- Am I prepared to devote the time and energy needed to attain my goals?

- What is the danger of success for me?

- Do I show any signs of the fear of success?

- Do any of my actions interfere with my progress toward my career goals?

- Am I prepared to adjust my career ambition?

TRUST
AS A BUILDING BLOCK
TO CORPORATE SUCCESS

HOW WOULD YOU HANDLE IT?

Consider each of the following situations. Place a check mark next to the action you think would be the best way to handle it. In the space provided, briefly explain the reasoning behind your choice. Compare your reactions to the answers at the end of this chapter after you finish reading.

1. Your subordinates are competent and experienced. However, you've noticed that the atmosphere in your department has become overly competitive. Colleagues refuse to cooperate with each other. Rumors and critical stories are common. Supervisors spend more time protecting their "territory" than productively working. Your first step should be to:

___ a. Limit communication between various sectors.

__ b. Encourage each supervisor to take a broader interest in the company as a whole.

__ c. Instigate more thorough training programs for supervisors.

__ d. Initiate a job description program to define more clearly each person's role in the organization.

_____

_____

_____

2. You have just been appointed interim manager in charge of a new department and plan to run it until a permanent manager can be found. You are unfamiliar with your immediate subordinates. They are wary of you as an outsider coming in to run their operations. Which of the following techniques would help establish a climate of trust?

__ a. Encourage your subordinates to understand and adopt your style of management.

__ b. Avoid revealing your feelings so that they won't suspect you of weakness.

__ c. Be vague about your management tactics so that you can evaluate each subordinate's style.

__ d. Have each subordinate explain his or her job to you and then ask how it could be improved.

_____

_____

_____

TRUST: WHAT IS IT?

Trust is different from confidence. Confidence is a function of judgment. You may be confident that your subordinates can carry out their assignments because you know they have the required skills. Trust is a feeling, freely experienced, without the qualification of evaluation. Though trust and confidence often occur together, trust is more fundamental. You experience it on an emotional rather than an intellectual level.

Trust is important to the proper functioning of groups— from families to business organizations to whole societies— as well as to the health of the individual.

Trust in the Business Environment

Trust is important to you as a manager because it opens up your creativity and spontaneity. It increases your energy by freeing you from burdensome worries. It helps reduce the stress of your job.

The larger value of trust in business lies in its effect on interpersonal relations. Trust between you and your subordinates and colleagues improves communication. It eliminates the question of motivation and the suspicion and undue competitiveness that can rob an organization of vitality. It lessens the amount of time and energy wasted in nonproductive controls and reporting systems. By promoting internal motivation, it reduces the need for external incentives.

To make people trustworthy, trust them. To make them untrustworthy, distrust them and show your distrust. When subordinates feel that you distrust them, they are likely to react with hostility and lack of responsibility, which further increases your distrust. When they perceive trust, they are more likely to identify with the goals of the company and attempt to justify that trust. Exhibit 7 illustrates how these spirals work.

THE FIRST STEP: TRUSTING YOURSELF

If you are unsure of yourself, you will rarely feel trust for another. A sense of hesitancy and lack of decisiveness will pervade your actions. You will never achieve the utmost effectiveness as a manager.

Self-trust in business occurs on two levels. First, you must trust your abilities. You must believe that you can cope with any situation or problem. This means recognizing the skills that are necessary for your job and that you already have, polishing those skills, and testing them regularly.

On a more fundamental level, self-trust includes a willingness to follow your intuition, your spontaneous judgment. Many managers are comfortable with their skills. Fewer are able to put total trust in their hunches and impulses. But the most effective managers do just that, because many business problems cannot be completely analyzed. Due to limited time or information, you have to act on how you feel about the situation. You can do that only if you are able to listen to and trust your intuition.

Here are five tips to help you develop self-trust:

1. *View yourself as unique.* Don't try to fit into a norm or mold. List ways in which your individual outlook and style contribute to the effectiveness of your performance.

EXHIBIT 7

Trust and Distrust Spirals

1. The Spiral of Distrust

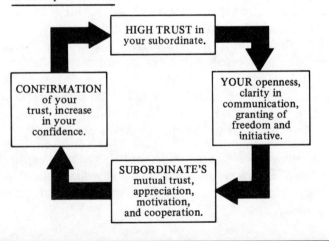

2. The Spiral of Trust

2. *Listen to your "inner voice."* Sometimes, all facts point to one decision, but something inside warns you against it. Pay attention to that voice.

3. *Review your abilities.* Any skill can become dull through lack of use. Which are the primary abilities you need in your current position? Are there any you could sharpen?

4. *Welcome responsibility.* Managers who rely too heavily on colleagues or subordinates never give their self-trust a chance to develop.

5. *Exercise your impulses.* If you never act spontaneously, you will never develop trust in your ability to do so. Deliberately act according to your impulses on occasion—in minor decision-making or a simple personal activity such as buying a new suit.

BUILDING YOUR TRUST IN OTHERS

Trusting yourself is not enough. As a manager, you are a competent, forceful, highly motivated individual. But too often, these admirable traits cause managers to become overly self-reliant. They no longer trust subordinates or colleagues to have the initiative and ability to work on their own. As a result, the effectiveness of the managers declines because they become too involved in the duties of others. Also, the morale and efficiency of the entire working group suffers.

In order to gauge your level of trust in your subordinates, colleagues, and others, turn to Exhibit 8 and take the Trust Assessment Survey.

To begin developing your trust of others, view each subordinate as an individual. Just as you should see yourself as unique, you must realize that every subordinate is, too. Consider each of the persons you work with. Ask yourself:

- How is each subordinate unique?

- What are each subordinate's strengths and weaknesses?

- What is different about the way each worker approaches the work?

- What special contributions could each one make?

- How does each subordinate handle his or her emotions?

- What moods does each person show regularly?

- What unrealized potentials does each worker have?

One manager, for example, was mistrustful of a competent subordinate because the latter was always negative about any new idea or change. The manager found this annoying and was uncertain about the subordinate's acceptance of new rules or procedures.

On reflection, the manager realized that the subordinate was not opposed to change. The subordinate's initial negative impulse was simply a personal idiosyncracy. In fact, that particular employee was as effective as any other. Looking at the situation in this way, the manager developed a feeling of complete trust in the subordinate.

TEN WAYS TO ENHANCE YOUR TRUST IN OTHERS

1. *Develop your personal interest.* To enhance the trust you feel toward key subordinates and colleagues, become interested in their personal lives. Casual mutual

EXHIBIT 8

Trust Assessment Survey

Think about a *particular* person with whom you work. Answer yes or no to each statement about that person. When you have finished, add up your score.

Completing the survey for a number of key subordinates and colleagues will give you a good overall picture of your trust level. Scoring follows the survey.

	Yes	**No**
1. This co-worker shares my view of the company's purpose.	____	____
2. The person is not as committed to goals as I am.	____	____
3. He or she is as honest as I am.	____	____
4. This colleague does not possess appropriate skills for the job.	____	____
5. He or she is straightforward and direct in communicating.	____	____
6. This person does not weigh his or her impulses carefully.	____	____
7. He or she understands readily when I explain something.	____	____
8. My colleague seems secretive about his or her personal life.	____	____
9. This person usually tries wholeheartedly to solve problems.	____	____
10. The colleague is interested mainly in his or her own advancement.	____	____
11. I can identify with the way this person feels about most situations.	____	____

	Yes	**No**
12. I would feel comfortable discussing personal matters with this co-worker.	____	____
13. This person possesses the initiative to work without close supervision.	____	____
14. This person's attitude is basically competitive rather than cooperative.	____	____
15. When I differ with this person, we are both open about our views.	____	____
16. This person would be shocked to know what I really think of him or her.	____	____
17. When I need help I know I can count on this colleague.	____	____
18. I hesitate to express negative feelings to my co-worker.	____	____
19. It is easy for me to be myself with this person.	____	____
20. I can imagine him or her committing a dishonest act.	____	____
21. This person always tries to make fair judgments.	____	____
22. He or she has a tendency to gossip about other people.	____	____
23. I feel relaxed when I am with this person.	____	____
24. He or she often needs guidance.	____	____
25. This person always holds up his or her end of a joint assignment.	____	____

Scoring

For odd-numbered statements: score **2** points for **Yes**;
                                        score **0** points for **No**.

For even-numbered statements: score **2** points for **No**;
                                        score **0** points for **Yes**.

Total Points

40 or more	high trust
30–40	average trust
20–30	low trust
Less than 20	distrust

---

inquiries about each other's families can strengthen the bond of trust you feel toward a subordinate.

2. *Recognize interdependence.* Make it clear that you wish to complement your colleagues, not compete against them. Share your insights and encourage them to do the same. Study the goals and aspirations you have in common. Emphasize the fact that teamwork is more effective than individual action.

3. *Help subordinates develop their skills.* If your distrust for a subordinate grows out of your feeling that the person is not capable of doing a good job, help the person to gain the necessary skills. Subordinates who doubt their own skills tend to avoid making suggestions, and they may misinterpret performance criteria. This perpetuates the cycle of distrust.

4. *Recognize differences in style.* There are many effective approaches to management. While you prefer one method, subordinates and colleagues may be equally

effective with a different approach. Sometimes, variations of style lead to distrust. Make sure that you agree with your subordinates on goals. Then let them handle matters in a way that suits their personality and style.

5. *Minimize labeling.* While job titles are useful in maintaining organizational efficiency, keep in mind that they are only words. Behind each label is a person. Avoid classification and coding except for administrative functions.

6. *Take risks.* To trust a person means to risk being disappointed. Recognize the risk and take it. It will pay off.

7. *Minimize interpersonal "strategies."* Management experts recommend many tactics and plans for dealing with other people. Consistently employing these impersonal strategies, however, rather than reacting spontaneously to the other person cuts down on trust.

8. *Consider context.* Don't focus only on a particular action and its consequences. All human beings are influenced by their background, social environment, and individual motives. Try to view each person's actions within that context. This enables you to better empathize with your subordinates and build your trust in them.

9. *Widen your interests.* The wider your cultural and intellectual pursuits, the better you can relate to the interests of others. The more multifaceted your personality, the easier it is to understand and trust others.

10. *Develop your generosity.* Generosity and flexibility aid in achieving insights. Both can create the positive element in empathy.

BUILDING OTHERS' TRUST IN YOU

The more you trust your subordinates and colleagues, the more likely they are to trust you—and one another. The benefits of mutual trust in any business organization are clear. Fear barriers that prevent candor and openness drop away. With trust, groups learn to gather data more quickly.

With the openness that is fostered with trust, there may well be more conflict and confrontation within a group. But it will be honest conflict that will lead to new ideas and creativity, not the suspicious and destructive conflict that can develop in an atmosphere of distrust.

Exhibit 9 offers guidelines for promoting others' trust in you.

FIVE BLOCKS TO MUTUAL TRUST

1. *Arbitrariness.* Trust is developed by relying on mutual consent rather than strict authority. If you dictate policies and procedures without giving reasons for them, your colleagues and subordinates will distrust you and view your future actions with uncertainty. Take time to "sell" your major policies to them. Be open to suggestions from others during decision-making. Be ready to reconsider any decisions that prove unsuccessful.

   For example, the marketing manger for a business equipment manufacturer concluded that the company's sales force could be improved by a nationwide recruiting campaign directed by the headquarters marketing staff. She informed her regional sales managers of this decision. Previously, the sales managers had had the authority to hire their own sales reps. They viewed the

EXHIBIT 9

Six Ways to Build Others' Trust in You

1. *Take responsibility.* Don't shift the blame for your actions and orders to a higher authority or to the system.

2. *Reveal your motivation.* If you want your subordinates to do something for the good of the company or your own career, be honest about it. Don't try to make them think that it is for their own good if it isn't.

3. *Play down your own role.* Exercise your authority, but don't abuse the privileges that your rank gives you. Create a cooperative atmosphere whenever possible.

4. *Build your understanding.* Work closely with your subordinates so they develop an understanding of how you think and how you approach difficulties. That way your subordinates will know what you'd expect them to do in a new situation. Talk to subordinates frequently about your thinking on specific problems. Let them know why you act the way you do. Help them see the situation from your perspective.

5. *Express your feelings.* "He's unpredictable." "I never know if she is satisfied with a project or not." "He seems to get mad suddenly." These are the types of complaints that subordinates make about uncommunicative superiors. If they don't know how you feel about things, they won't trust your reactions. If you are happy or dissatisfied, worried or impressed, don't hide your feelings. By revealing your emotions, you will become more predictable to your colleagues, and more human as well. Their empathy will reinforce their trust.

6. *Use intrinsic motivation.* Encouraging your subordinates to be motivated by their own interest and pride in their work is a far more direct route to trust than relying on punishment or financial incentives.

decision as an incursion on their authority. They became distrustful of the marketing executive, wondering what other prerogatives she might take from them next.

A better way for the marketing manager to have handled this situation would have been to call in the sales managers and discuss the idea of improved recruiting with them. She should have asked for suggestions and mentioned her own ideas. In this way, she could have pointed out that she was interested only in improving the quality of the sales force and that her action did not represent a lessening of the managers' authority.

2. *Inconsistency.* While your decisions should not be arbitrary, neither should they be inconsistent. The manager who vacillates or shows differing standards in various situations will not be trusted by subordinates or colleagues. Regularly review the principles behind your management style and make sure you apply them consistently.

3. *Ambiguity.* Ambiguity on the part of a manager creates uncertainty, tension, and mistrust in other people. Ambiguity can result from a lack of clarity in communications, uncertainty about a policy, or an attempt to avoid the responsibility of making a definite decision. Eliminate ambiguity by evaluating policies thoroughly before communicating them to your subordinates.

4. *Defensiveness.* Managers who are not willing to admit their mistakes or who try to cover up errors or shift the blame generate mistrust in their colleagues. It is better to admit your failures than to defend yourself when you are wrong. Such honesty generates empathy and trust in your colleagues. Encourage your subordinates, in turn, to admit and learn from their errors rather than

cover them up. Don't be punitive with subordinates who are open about their mistakes and willing to rectify them.

5. *Negative Assumptions.* Making negative assumptions about your subordinates can become self-fulfilling. The subordinates sense your lack of confidence in them and act in such a way that your assumption seems justified. The following attitudes may reflect negative assumptions you have made about your subordinates or colleagues:

- "They don't really know what's best for them."

- "They're unsure exactly what they want."

- "They need guidance in performing their jobs."

- "I must take the initiative or they will do nothing."

- "They are not motivated; they're only seeking the easiest course."

- "They aren't interested in learning or developing."

TRUST AND DELEGATION OF AUTHORITY

In no other area of business is trust as vitally important as in the delegation of authority. If you do not trust your subordinates, you are unlikely to give them the freedom and responsibility needed for effective delegation. And if they do not feel a sense of mutual trust, they are unlikely to act with the autonomy necessary to carry out their delegated duties.

Trust allows you to assign complete, open-ended tasks to your subordinates, thus relieving yourself of a great deal of unnecessary work and worry. And it allows subordinates to act independently, encouraging them to increase their management skills and develop their capacity for self-directed work.

Symptoms of Lack of Trust

There are four principal warning signs that point to the absence of trust in delegation of authority.

1. *Checking with the boss.* If your subordinates are continually returning to ask your approval of projects you have delegated to them, either they are afraid you won't back up their authority on these matters or they don't know how you expect them to handle the work.

2. *Involvement in subordinates' jobs.* If you frequently become involved in the details of tasks that you've delegated, you are telling your subordinates that you really don't trust them. Effective delegation means that you agree with your subordinates on the results expected; then leave them to complete the task in the way they feel is best.

3. *Impaired information flow.* Withholding information that your subordinates need to facilitate their assignment is a certain sign that you lack trust. They should receive all necessary data and should not have to request information or continually ask questions.

4. *Disorganization.* Unclear or overlapping areas of responsibility, duplication of efforts, and general confusion on the part of a subordinate are all symptoms of your lack of trust.

TRUST IN THE ORGANIZATION

Trust among members of your company can help to make the organization more productive. Trust encourages people to work toward shared goals rather than out of self-interest. It encourages the flow of communication within the company, resulting in more ideas, more creativity, and more cooperation.

You can use one or more of these standard management practices to help develop a trusting atmosphere in your organization.

- *Information*. Provide employees with plenty of data on the company goals and progress to increase their involvement.

- *Reduce barriers*. Encourage more communication among departments and people who are now isolated from one another. Break down channels of communication that are now too rigid.

- *Freedom*. Allow employees to discover their own work and rest rhythms by eliminating prescribed breaks. Get rid of time clocks. Institute flexible work schedules.

- *Teams*. Build mutual trust and employees' identity with the company by grouping them into teams and task forces.

- *Appraisals*. Reduce the strictness and secrecy of performance appraisals. Allow employees to participate more actively in their own evaluation.

- *Segmentation*. Don't formulate duties that restrict employees to only a single limited job. Encourage employees to develop a broad view of the company.

- *Rules*. Eliminate petty and annoying regulations that are not vital to operations or safety.

- *Competition*. Avoid destructive competition among departments. Eliminate budget warfare in which departments fight over resources.

- *Career development*. Open up routes of advancement for employees. Provide training opportunities for those who want them.

PUTTING TRUST IN PERSPECTIVE

Your principal goal is to use your power as a manager to accomplish the objectives of your company. Trusting your subordinates and colleagues does not mean abdicating that responsibility.

Properly used, trust can widen your power. Trust makes your subordinates more effective and increases their initiative. It frees you to attack your own responsibilities with greater energy.

In order to make sure you use trust properly, consider the following three rules:

1. Never lose sight of the fact that trust is a useful emotion. It helps to get things done; it makes your job easier; it can make you more effective. It is not an end in itself.

2. Never let trust prevent you from giving advice or guidance to subordinates when you feel that it is needed.

3. Never use trust as a tool to gain favor with subordinates or as a means of manipulating them. Trust is a serious matter and attempts to use it in a manipulative way will inevitably work against you.

ANSWERS:
HOW WOULD YOU HANDLE IT?

1. The best answer is *b*. Taking a wider view of the company helps supervisors to be more trusting and cooperative and less self-centered. They see that only by working together can they all benefit. Limited communication and more strictly defining jobs only increase distrust. Training does not influence the emotional sphere of the manager's activity.

2. The best answer is *d*. You will gain greater understanding of the department and show your new subordinates that you are interested in them and trust them to make recommendations about their responsibilities. By encouraging your subordinates to adopt your style of management, you ignore their uniqueness. Hiding your feelings discourages empathy and trust. Ambiguous management tactics break down rather than build trust.

COUNTERACTING THE
NEGATIVE EFFECTS OF ENVY
IN YOUR ORGANIZATION

HOW WOULD YOU HANDLE IT?

Consider each of the following situations. Place a check mark next to the action you think would be the best way to handle it. In the space provided, briefly explain the reasoning behind your choice. Compare your reactions to the answers at the end of this chapter after you finish reading.

1. As the manager of the company's operations department, you have a number of supervisors reporting to you. One of them in particular is a valued and trusted aide. He has done a superb job for you over the years. Recently a younger but experienced supervisor joined your staff and developed a new operational technique that saved all sorts of money. Much praise and recognition have been heaped on the newcomer.

   You realize that the young supervisor's achievement is beginning to overshadow that of your other close aide.

What is the best way to sidetrack any envy your aide may feel?

— a. Tell your aide that the new idea was not really as valuable as everyone seemed to think.

— b. Give the newcomer an assignment that will prove he is not as competent as others think.

— c. Point out to your aide that the new man is bringing a fresh perspective and that maybe everyone can learn from him.

— d. Explain that this is just beginner's luck and that the new supervisor won't be able to keep coming up with good ideas.

_____

_____

_____

_____

2. Your company is moving to new quarters. You have to assign offices to a group of subordinates who are all relatively equal in the company hierarchy. Some rooms have excellent views, others are less desirable, a few are even windowless. You want to assign the offices in a way that minimizes the envy felt by those who are given the less desirable offices. What would be your best approach?

— a. Give the desirable offices to those individuals who would most appreciate the view.

— b. Assign the rooms strictly on the basis of merit,

with the more productive people being awarded the more desirable offices.

___ c.   Place those employees who have the most potential in the more pleasant offices.

___ d.   Use a lottery system to assign offices.

_____

_____

_____

_____

WHAT IS ENVY?

Envy is the feeling of discontent and ill will that a person feels in relation to an advantage or honor possessed by another. It is a directed emotion. With no target, it does not occur. Envious persons must direct their feelings against others as a result of what they perceive as the others' advantage over themselves.

Envy most often occurs between persons at relatively equal levels of accomplishment because, in order to envy, people must generally feel deprived of the advantage, must feel that it could just as well have been theirs as the other's. Production workers, for example, are not likely to envy the president of the company, but they may envy the privileges of their immediate superiors.

Unlike the other emotions discussed in this book, envy is completely negative. It cannot be turned into an asset; it has to be eliminated. Envy should not be mistaken for the feeling of competitiveness that spurs a person to work harder in order to match or beat the efforts of a successful co-worker. Instead, envy prompts workers to undermine the success of others.

THE NEGATIVE EFFECTS OF ENVY

Envy diminishes the person who experiences it and causes divisiveness and disruption within an organization. Here are ways that envy can adversely affect you and your organization:

- A colleague envies you and reduces his cooperation with you.

- A manager envies a subordinate in training and fails to give him the proper guidance.

- Subordinates waste time discussing imagined inequalities related to those they envy.

- A subordinate declines to push enthusiastically for a new idea because its success will generate the envy of his peers.

- Petty squabbling over privileges reduces communication and effective organized efforts.

- Groups form, reducing intra-company cooperation.

- Malicious rumors generated by envy hurt a manager's career and reduce his motivation.

- Status becomes more important than substance.

- A foreman is envious of the incentive pay being won by his productive subordinates. So he limits the bonuses and reduces productivity.

THE SOURCE OF ENVY

The primary source of envy is inequality. Envious people see that someone else has more than they do—more money, power, privilege, honor, happiness, ability, or anything else. They then imagine that they themselves could be enjoying that advantage. They unconsciously consider that the other person's good fortune has deprived them. They become resentful and focus their negative feeling on the other.

Self-esteem plays a large role in envy. Those who experience the emotion suffer from either too high or too low a view of themselves. If they are insecure in their own abilities, they see every accomplishment by another as a threat to their status. If they are arrogant, they feel that they deserve every advantage before another. In both cases, the result is envy.

THE SYMPTOMS OF ENVY

The most direct symptom of envy is an open feeling or expression of dislike. But envy is often not so direct. It may surface in a general personal dislike for another for which reasons other than envy are given: the person is rude, boring, unattractive, or disloyal, for instance. But envy may well be at the root of those feelings.

Envy can come to light in the way people talk about a successful person. They may downplay the person's achievements. Or they may claim that those accomplishments are the result of mere luck. They may hint that the successful person had an unfair advantage, or that success implies low motives or dishonesty. They may tell stories about the person, true or untrue, that are designed to counteract the advantage he or she has attained.

Envy sometimes wears even more complicated disguises. For example, a supervisor may advise a subordinate whom he envies that she should lower her ambitions, that she's taking too much of a risk by her actions. Or the supervisor, alternatively, may urge the subordinate to overextend herself, hoping that she will eventually fail.

In an organization, envy also may appear in the form of closed groups that are antagonistic toward each other. It also comes out as malicious gossip or slander. In the end, envy within an organization breeds conformity; no one wants to risk the enmity of his or her fellows by outstanding achievement. As a manager, you must learn to handle three types of envy: the envy others feel toward you, organizational envy, and the envy you may feel toward others.

HANDLING THE ENVY OTHERS FEEL TOWARD YOU

Managers are often the object of the envy of both subordinates and colleagues. The achievements necessary to attain your current position, and the privileges that go with it, are natural instigators for the envy of others. In some senses, being envied is the price of success.

In order to diminish the envy of your subordinates, you must approach them carefully. To berate them for their feeling will only add to their sense of injustice and fuel their envy. Use a positive rather than a negative approach. Take them aside occasionally and praise them for some concrete achievement they have made. Let them know that you are aware of their efforts and interested in their advancement. This will be much more likely to diminish their envy than punishing or ignoring them would be.

Sometimes, subordinates become envious simply because they feel they are being excluded from the decision-making process. Sit down with these people and listen to their ideas. Ask them to recommend changes. Even if you don't act on their suggestions, they will gain a sense of participation that may reduce their envy.

Your basic reaction to the envy of others should be twofold. First, you should not let envy halt your own efforts to achieve. If you avoid standing out, constrain your abilities, tone down your new ideas, refuse deserved awards and recognition, or in any other way moderate your success for fear that your colleagues or subordinates will envy you, you will do both yourself and your company a disservice. Success can generate respect and emulation as well as envy. At the same time, you should avoid unnecessarily creating envy in others through your actions.

Here are four ways to moderate the envy you encounter in others:

1. Humility can sidetrack the envy of others. Boasting of an accomplishment will be perceived by an envious person as "rubbing it in," and that can fuel hostility. Remember that arrogance stimulates envy. Take a reasonably modest attitude toward your achievements. Don't imply that you feel they make you a superior person. A modest attitude can change envy to respect.

2. Helpfulness is an excellent way to counter envy. Display your willingness to help others achieve. Aide a colleague during a particularly busy time. Offer sound advice to a subordinate about a difficult problem.

3. Share the credit when possible. Give subordinates and colleagues their share of credit for your own achieve-

ments. Emphasize the fact that success is the result of a team effort. Thank them for their help.

4. **Don't flaunt your privileges.** Do not unnecessarily call the attention of subordinates to privileges they do not share. For example, do not take a two-hour lunch break if your immediate subordinates are limited to a half-hour.

ELIMINATING ORGANIZATIONAL ENVY

Envy works against the very purpose of a business organization. Instead of leading to trust, cooperation, creativity, and productivity, it generates distrust, hostility, conformity, and wasted energy. If you discover the signs of envy in your organization—cliques, false rumors, covert antagonism—you can take these eight steps to help alleviate it:

1. *Encourage openness.* A closed and secretive environment nurtures envy. Keep subordinates informed of the reasons for decisions, particularly about promotions and the awarding of privileges. Head off rumors by publicizing any changes in policy or procedure in advance. Call subordinates into open meetings where they can discuss their grievances with total candor. Set up formal, effective grievance procedures and keep them open to all employees.

2. *Discourage conformity.* Envy tends to level achievement. Make sure all your subordinates know that the company values outstanding achievement and originality. Set up brainstorming and other idea sessions to

encourage every member of the organization to contribute.

3. *Eliminate undue privileges.* Even well-meant policies can cause problems if they foster envy. Many companies, for example, treat outside consultants with more deference and respect than they treat their own managers, or give staff executives more privileges than their counterparts in line positions. Always be on the alert for undue privileges and eliminate them.

4. *Tolerate mistakes.* When the creative person makes a mistake, the envious person will try to draw attention to it. If you take a harsh view of all errors, you will encourage the same attitude in your subordinates. This will discourage those who possess creativity and originality. Advise subordinates to learn from their mistakes rather than suffer over them.

5. *Be fair.* Although envious people view with hostility even the well-deserved rewards of others, their feelings are heightened by unfair advantages. If a subordinate is given an honor he or she really does not deserve, the envy of the entire organization is aroused.

While it is impossible to run a business totally on democratic principles, use a consensus approach to decisions when appropriate. For example, if each of a group of ten engineers is eligible to represent the company at a conference, sit down with the group. Decide through a vote or discussion who they think is the best candidate.

Or use pure chance to make a decision. A lottery system can be used to assign either advantageous or undesirable duties. No one considers the winner of a lottery prize with hostile envy since no one is more deserving to win a chance drawing than another.

Other methods for maintaining fairness include rotating duties, using a strict seniority system, and letting groups of subordinates decide among themselves how they will divide responsibilities.

6. *Promote equal opportunity.* Subordinates will be less envious of others' achievements if they realize that they had an equal chance to succeed. Let everyone in the organization compete through objective testing and merit scales for the opportunities to advance or enter training programs. Whenever convenient, open educational courses and seminars to everyone. Use a formalized system to consider promotion candidates rather than relying on arbitrary or strictly personal standards.

At the same time, keep in mind that equality of opportunity should not aim for equality of achievement. Your approach should not require that you lower the quality of the training programs or discourage those who excel.

7. *Use quiet rewards.* While well-deserved public awards and honors can be useful incentives in a company, you can reduce envy by keeping them to a minimum. Instead, call in a subordinate for a private talk if that person has performed well. Express the company's recognition and appreciation of his or her efforts. But discourage the subordinate from boasting about the distinction to fellow workers. This type of recognition can be very useful to encourage outstanding subordinates without generating the envy of their peers.

8. *Encourage teamwork.* The more successfully you can promote a joint effort on the part of your subordinates, the less envy they will feel. Small teams, committees, and task forces give rise to a feeling of group rather than individual achievement. Even pairing two subor-

dinates to work together reduces the envy others might feel toward the success of a single individual.

ADDRESSING YOUR OWN ENVY

If you discover that you are envious of another, you should attempt to replace the feeling with one of respect. At the first indication of envy, try to determine exactly what it is about the person that you envy: personality, salary, job success, creativity? Then ask yourself if this is a quality or advantage you would like to have. Finally, ask yourself how the person's example can help you to achieve this advantage. What can you learn from the person you envy? In this way, you allow your respect for the person to benefit you rather than letting your envy diminish you.

Here are some suggestions for combating your envy:

- *Learn to identify with others.* Instead of closing yourself off from people who achieve, try to identify with their success, participate in their happiness. Look for ways in which the success of one person benefits all.

- *Boost your self-esteem.* The greater your feeling of self-worth, the less susceptible you will be to envy. The checklist in Exhibit 10 will help you evaluate your level of self-esteem.

- *De-emphasize awards.* While achievement is a real and important part of business life, the honors and prizes that sometimes go with it are much less meaningful. In fact, many awards and honors have as much to do with the awarding group's personal preferences as they do with real accomplishment.

EXHIBIT 10

A Checklist to Help You Measure Your Self-Esteem

Mark each statement Agree or Disagree:

_____Achievement is not my major goal.

_____Being a gracious winner is as important to me as winning.

_____Modesty will often win more advantages than boasting will.

_____My achievements speak for themselves.

_____Another's success in no way diminishes mine.

_____The work I do has value in itself, not just for the rewards it brings.

_____I have unique qualities not possessed in exactly the same combination by anyone else.

_____Specific failures have nothing to do with my real value.

_____My view of myself does not depend on the opinions of others.

_____I am confident of my ability to cope with difficulties.

_____I rarely have negative thoughts about myself.

_____I am making the best possible use of my talents and abilities.

Scoring

If you disagree with more than five of these statements, your self-esteem is low and you are likely to be susceptible to envy. Examine each statement you disagree with and ask yourself why you have this attitude.

ANSWERS:
HOW WOULD YOU HANDLE IT?

1. The best answer is *c*. Substitute your respect for envy. Draw some advantage for yourself and your people from the newcomer's success, instead of downplaying it. To undervalue the new man's achievement, to await his eventual failure, or try to bring it about will only increase the chances of envy.

2. The best choice is answer *d*. A lottery system will eliminate the complaint that you played favorites or practiced discrimination. Any other way of assigning the offices introduces a question of judgment which leaves an opening for envy.

7

TURNING GUILT
INTO AN EMOTIONAL
ADVANTAGE

HOW WOULD YOU HANDLE IT?

Consider each of the following situations. Place a check mark next to the action you think would be the best way to handle it. In the space provided, briefly explain the reasoning behind your choice. Compare your reactions to the answers at the end of the chapter after you finish reading.

1. Dave Barry and Ed Palmer were both middle managers in a large textile company. They had started with the company at the same time and had been friends for many years. When a vice-presidency opened up in their company, both men were eligible for promotion. Dave was offered the position. He knew that he was qualified to take on the responsibilities. However, he felt his friend Ed was just as qualified, if not more so. The prospect of being Ed's superior after all those years as equals, and of taking a job that Ed could just as well

have had, made Dave feel guilty. How should he handle this feeling?

___ a.   Break off all contact with his former colleague so as to put the matter out of his mind and lessen his guilt.

___ b.   Apologize to Ed Palmer.

___ c.   Say nothing, accept the position, and do as good a job as possible.

___ d.   Refuse the position and recommend that Palmer be appointed instead.

_____

_____

_____

2.   Jim Harding was the sales manager for an auto products company. While in another city visiting a prospective client, he ran into several old friends whom he hadn't seen in years. He invited his friends out for a night on the town, including an expensive dinner and show. He charged all the costs to his company expense account. After the vouchers were submitted and approved, Harding had second thoughts. He had often reprimanded his subordinates for exactly this type of activity. Now he felt guilty for doing it himself. What should he do?

___ a.   Live with the guilt in order to avoid any damage to his reputation.

___ b.   Report lower expenses than he incurs on some trip in the future in order to even the account.

___ c.   Go to the company controller, explain that he now

realizes the expenses were not justified, and reimburse the company.

__ d.   Rationalize the action by saying that charging personal expenses to the company is not really wrong if it goes undetected.

_____

_____

_____

_____

WHAT IS GUILT?

Guilt is a personal emotion. It comes from within. It arises when your actions clash with your sense of right and wrong. Guilt usually has few outward symptoms. It is not one of the emotions—like fear or anger—that prepare you to act quickly. Rather, it is like trust—an inclination, an inner sense. It can be a strong feeling, even an excruciating one, and can have profound effects on your adjustment to life. But its manifestation is almost always internal and psychological.

Guilt is commonly confused with fear. Fear indeed can be related to guilt in that you have done something wrong and fear that the act will be discovered. This feeling is a common one.

You drive faster than the speed limit. You file an inaccurate tax return. You take a few days of sick leave when you are not really ill. When the possibility of discovery arises, you might feel guilty about what you have done, or be afraid of the consequences if you are found out.

In other words, fear and guilt can exist together. You may genuinely feel that you have done wrong, you may want to make amends, but you are still afraid of the consequences of admitting your guilt. This is one of the principal sources of conflict in handling guilt. This feeling can give rise to profound self-searching, examination of values, and the need to accept the unpleasant consequences of guilt.

ORIGINS OF GUILT

One source of guilt is the moral training of childhood. Guilt begins as guilty fear. Gradually, this fear is internalized. The punishment no longer comes from outside but from the inner conscience. In the mature personality, this internalization goes even further. You may develop what psychologists call an ego ideal. This is an image of yourself as you feel you should be. When you act in a way that violates this ego ideal, your image of yourself is fractured; it is no longer a coherent whole. This condition, with its accompanying discomfort, is called guilt.

Guilt exists until the fracture is repaired—through reparation, confession, or atonement—or until you revise your ego ideal to such an extent that your action is congruent with the altered image of yourself. If neither of these courses is taken, the guilt stays with you.

Guilt is not determined entirely by the ethical strictures of childhood, however. It also depends on cues you receive from the behavior of others. For example, you may once have believed that it is wrong to cheat on taxes, to inflate your expense account, to drive faster than the speed limit. Later on, though, the realization that "everyone does these things" may assuage your guilt and eventually eliminate it. This is a common occurrence in business. Certain unethical practices—bribery, for example—become the norm in an industry. Managers who would otherwise feel guilty about the activity come to accept it as standard practice.

Guilt depends on your ever-changing view of yourself. Your ethical concerns become more sophisticated as you mature. Your sense of guilt alters. You absorb new ideas from religion, law, and other sytems of ethics. Guilt can become inappropriate. You can become too strict with yourself. You may develop guilt over values you don't really believe in. According to Gary Tuckman, a New Jersey psychologist, guilt can be a blanket that suffocates us and keeps us from growing and developing, or a moral framework in which we can find new experience and become more fully human.

Guilt is an integral mechanism in the functioning of the individual in his or her ethical environment and also in society as a system of personal interactions. As a manager, you regularly make a wide range of decisions that affect the lives of many people. You set policies that have a long-range impact on your company and on those it comes in contact with. Because of this, you need a sense of right and wrong that is extremely coherent and incisive. You need the signals that guilt provides to help guide your actions.

According to Dr. Tuckman, guilt "is a warning buzzer that tells us 'look twice, this is an important area in your emotional life.' We should neither ignore this feeling, nor allow it to direct us blindly. The adult response is to open a dialogue within the self, consider the alternatives, and make a choice."

GUILT AND MATURITY

Genuine guilt is a sign of emotional maturity. It means that you have developed ethical standards on which to base your choices and for which you no longer have to look outside yourself for guidance. In many ways, healthy guilt defines your relationship with your company. It allows you to act in ways that are acceptable to other employees. It guides you back to the right track when you stray from acceptable courses of conduct.

Though the idea of competition between companies sometimes obscures the fact, ethics based on guilt are essential for the efficient functioning of all business. Every good manager recognizes that competition is not "to the death" and knows that the health of the company depends on healthy industry.

Managers recognize that to attack their competitors unethically, to harm the public good, to exploit their employees is not only wrong, but is poor business strategy. They know that social responsibility is not only the duty of every executive but also a pathway to success.

Guilt and the ethical choices from which it springs define how you live your life. It constitutes the foundation of your character and the guiding principles of your actions. For this reason, you should recognize guilt for what it is and take advantage of the feeling rather than think of it as an impediment.

THE RELATION OF GUILT AND ETHICS

Ethics are a matter for each person to determine within the context of the culture and value system. Law, custom, religion, philosophical beliefs, and the example of others all go into building each person's system of ethics.

In the modern world, guilt has become not only a product of ethics but also a determining factor in making ethical decisions. Some people have decided that what they feel emotionally to be wrong is wrong and that what does not give rise to guilt is not wrong. Those who adhere to more traditional ethical standards, of course, disagree.

The complex and rapid changes that have affected people in the twentieth century have resulted in the waning influence of traditional standards. In their place have arisen "situational ethics," which provide few rigid rules of behavior. Instead, the individual decides what is right in each situation. Ethical standards are improvised based on certain general principles of behavior. The use of situational ethics is a more subjective way of approaching moral questions. It requires you to ask several questions. Under what circumstances are you doing something? Why are you doing it? How are you doing it? The three questions are interrelated, and the answers to all three help you decide whether your action is right or wrong.

BUSINESS ETHICS

Ethics in business present the same difficulties as ethics in private life. In some senses, as a manager, you confront even more trying problems in your business conduct. First, changes in the business environment are rapid.

- Improvements in data processing can open up new questions of privacy.

- Changing attitudes of workers raise questions of power and authority.

- Increasing international trade brings the company into contact with other cultures and moral systems.

Second, your actions as a manager carry even greater moral responsibility than those in your private life. Errors in business can affect your colleagues, your company, and the community as a whole. You cannot avoid wielding con-

siderable power. And great power implies profound responsibility.

Finally, as a manager, you have to pay attention not
only to your personal code of ethics and that of society, but
also to the regulations that govern business affairs, the cus-
toms and practices of your particular industry, and the policies of your own company. Sometimes, you may have to
balance one set of values against another. A practice accepted in your industry and beneficial to your company may
be immoral by your personal standards. Careful consideration is needed to avoid later guilt.

As a manager, you should play a vital role in maintaining your company's policies. Make certain that all your
subordinates and workers know what the company rules are.
Display them in writing so that all can read them.

HOW TO HANDLE GUILT

The first step toward eliminating inappropriate guilt from
your work life and taking advantage of adaptive guilt is to
start a "guilt record." This is a simple way to find out how
guilt operates in your life and to identify inappropriate guilt.
Exhibit 11 shows you how to set up a guilt record.

You should also review this ten-point program to help
you eliminate problems that you may be encountering with
guilt.

1. *Recognize guilt.* Unrecognized guilt can become a serious problem. It is frequently found to be the cause of
   neurosis. The problem is that even though your conscious mind is not aware of guilt, it works in your
   subconscious, sapping your energy and damaging your
   self-esteem. You expend additional energy keeping the
   guilt from rising to the surface of your consciousness.

EXHIBIT 11

A Sample Managerial Guilt Record

You don't need to maintain a guilt record all the time. Use it when you are troubled by feelings of guilt. You may also turn to it occasionally as a self-monitor. The very fact that it allows you to identify and analyze the role that guilt plays in your life makes the guilt record a most useful tool for the adoptive use of guilt.

To keep a guilt record, use a convenient notebook. Jot down any guilt feelings you have or any actions that are ethically ambiguous or could give rise to guilt. Study the two examples offered below. Then answer the following questions about the guilty thought or act.

1. What specifically do I feel guilty about?_____
   _____
   _____

2. If my feeling of guilt is the result of an ambiguous ethic, what is that ethic?_____
   _____

3. Is my view realistic? (Explain.)_____
   _____

4. What values have I transgressed?_____
   _____
   _____

5. What options are open to me for handling the guilt?_____
   _____
   _____

6. How can I learn from this experience?_____
   _____
   _____

Example:

"I feel guilty for not helping out a colleague when I knew she was burdened with work and I was not."

Realistic: This is a fair assessment of the situation, though I did have work to do; I wasn't completely idle.

Value: I believe that it is right to lend a hand to a colleague who needs it, particularly because this colleague has helped me out several times.

Options: I can apologize to her and look for an occasion to help her in the future.

Learn: I should make it a rule to always help a colleague who is overworked.

Example:

"I feel guilty for telling my research staff that its work on that new product was all in vain because the company is scrapping its plans to introduce it."

Realistic: Though the researchers were extremely disappointed by the news, I am really taking too much of the blame. The decision to end the project was not mine alone.

Value: Ideally it would be nice if everyone's work should come to fruition. I should realize, though, that this is not always possible.

Options: All I can do is express my sympathy to the researchers. I really should not feel guilty.

Learn: I must be careful not to base my guilt just on sympathy with others when I have done nothing wrong.

2. *Evaluate your behavior*. Surprisingly enough, one of the most common sources of guilt is ongoing behavior. For example, say a supplier has fallen into the habit of sending you an expensive gift each time you place an order with him. You feel guilty because it is against company rules for you to accept such gifts, but you continue to accept them. You rationalize your behavior by saying that the supplier would be offended if you refused. Take some time to think the matter out. If you genuinely feel you are doing wrong, tactfully end the behavior.

3. *Analyze your values*. Regularly consider the values that give rise to your guilt. Ask yourself several questions: On what foundation do I base my system of ethics? How do I feel that I should treat other people? What are my feelings about the practices in my industry? What are my feelings about the policies and rules of my company?

4. *Make restitution for wrongs*. Some managers suffer from guilt because they refuse to act in the way that their guilt prompts them to act. If you openly recognize that you have done wrong, your first step should be to rectify the damage you've done. If you've injured someone's reputation, do what you can to restore it. This is the most direct way both to assuage the pain you feel from your guilt and to use your guilt to help you grow.

5. *Don't hide your guilt*. Guilt rises to inappropriate levels and does the most damage when it remains hidden. Exposure takes away much of the power of inappropriate guilt to inflict pain. It also often shows guilt to be exaggerated in regard to the wrong you've done.

6. *Don't use guilt as justification*. Some managers take the attitude that if they feel guilty about something, then they are absolved of part of the responsibility. They continue to act in the same way or to ignore the consequences of their actions. They feel that guilt wipes away blame. This can become a rationalization for continuing guilt-producing behavior.

7. *Avoid remorse.* In some cases, guilt can rise to despondency, paralysis of action, and finally depression. This is why it is important to act on your guilt—through internal analysis, interpersonal discussion, restitution, and change of behavior.

8. *Increase your generosity.* Managers sometimes feel guilty about their own good fortune. One way to handle this type of inappropriate guilt is to become more generous in your dealings with others, whether sharing knowledge and insight, delegating power, or improving conditions at work.

9. *Forget the past.* Managers sometimes feed on regrets about the past. Clearly face the fact that past events can never be changed. You can only act in the present.

10. *Be forgiving.* If you are quick to forgive wrongs committed against you and to overlook the shortcomings of others, you will be better able to handle your own guilt.

The next two chapters deal with problem areas that often result from a mishandling of the basic emotions: anger, joy, guilt, and so forth. Anxiety and depression are not emotions in themselves, but are part of the emotional framework of many people's overall psychological makeup.

The difference between the two is often one of degree, with anxiety being the less severe. It is usually easier to handle the problems associated with anxiety, and many of the suggestions in Chapter 8 will work for you. Depression, on the other hand, generally demands more expertise and guidance. If you have any questions about the value of a self-help activity, you should seek professional help.

ANSWERS:
HOW WOULD YOU HANDLE IT?

1. The best answer is *c*. The guilt that Barry feels is inappropriate. He has won a promotion in a fair contest. There is no reason for him to apologize or to refuse the appointment. To avoid contact with his former colleague would keep this inappropriate guilt alive.

2. The best answer is *c*. To make reparations to the company should completely eliminate Harding's guilt. To try to live with it would be to deny his own values. To try to atone by reporting lower expenses on another trip is not appropriate when direct reparation is possible. While it might be possible to review his values later, for Harding to deny that his behavior is wrong after reprimanding his subordinates for it would be self-serving and would not help him deal with his guilt.

8

TURNING ANXIETY
INTO A POTENT
MANAGERIAL FORCE

HOW WOULD YOU HANDLE IT?

Consider the following situations. Place a check mark next
to the action you think would be the best way to handle
each problem. In the space provided, briefly explain the
reasoning behind your choices. Compare your reactions to
the answers at the end of the chapter after you finish reading.

1. Ann Lanson is a manager in a large financial services
   company. She performs her duties efficiently and enjoys
   her work. However, for the past year, since her promotion to her current position, she has experienced a
   vague uneasiness. She frequently imagines that despite
   her effectiveness, she is not capable of performing her
   job. Thoughts of potential disasters have crept into her
   consciousness. She has begun to put in longer hours of
   work, sometimes remaining at her desk until late at
   night. She has become exhausted and now dreads going

to work each morning. What would be Ann's best course of action to resolve this situation?

___ a.   Cut back on the hours she works and take more vacations.

___ b.   Review her career goals.

___ c.   Seek a transfer to a position with fewer responsibilities.

___ d.   Tell herself to stop worrying and enjoy life more.

_____

_____

_____

2.   You are the manager in charge of your company's research and development department. Lately you have encountered morale problems among your staff. Some have complained that they are under too much pressure to produce new products. Turnover has increased. Some loyal workers seem irritable and easily angered. Engineers are critical of each other. There is a general sense of pessimism and cynicism in the department. How can you restore morale and productivity among these subordinates?

___ a.   Replace the time constraints on the subordinates with more flexible deadlines.

___ b.   Let groups and task forces remain intact and move from project to project.

___ c.   Provide an outlet, such as a grievance session, in which employees could express their feelings about their work.

___ d.   All of the above.

_____

_____

_____

WHAT IS ANXIETY?

The American Psychiatric Association defines anxiety as "apprehension, tension, or uneasiness that stems from anticipation of danger, the cause of which is unknown." This definition includes two important aspects of anxiety. First, the object of anxiety is always vague, often unknown. You feel uneasy about some area of your life, but not about any one particular event or object. This is what distinguishes anxiety from fear, which is always directed toward a definite object. The second point about anxiety is that it is anticipatory. You feel anxiety about the future, not about the present. Confronted with an immediate danger, you may feel fear, but you will not feel anxious.

Both these aspects make anxiety difficult to deal with. Since it has no definite object, you cannot, as you can with fear, unlearn your anxiety through exposure to the object. And since it is marked by anticipation, events and thoughts in the present often have little effect on it.

Anxiety may invoke many of the same symptoms as fear and anger. Like them, it is a physical preparation to marshall and use energy. Your heart speeds up, your mouth turns dry, your breathing becomes shallow, muscles tighten and may tremble. Prolonged, mild anxiety can exist, though, with few of these overt symptoms. You may feel only a vague sense of threat, an apprehension you cannot quite put a name to.

ANXIETY IN BUSINESS

Anxiety is the result of nonspecific pressures. For the manager, these pressures are more prevalent today than ever before. They constantly or periodically weigh on your mind. While they vary depending on your position and industry, many are common to almost all managers.

Anxiety is not always negative. For the manager dealing with uncertainty and conflicting pressures every day, it can become a normal feeling. You can best adapt to anxiety if you expect it and recognize its potential sources. Here are the seven major conditions that give rise to anxiety in business.

1. *Time pressure.* The pace of modern business grows ever faster. Demands for new products, changes in markets and resource supplies, deadlines, seasonal rushes—all these and more put pressure on you to work more quickly. Delayed reactions to events can be disastrous. This accelerated pace is a prime instigator of anxiety.

2. *Evaluation.* More companies are closely scrutinizing managers to see how they use their time and to rate their contributions to the company. Some people find it hard to deal with the greater emphasis on managerial evaluation and productivity.

3. *Health.* Many managers are at an age when health concerns are becoming more important than ever before. A heart attack in a certain group threatens every colleague of the man or woman who has it.

4. *Inner conflict.* While struggling to be successful, managers are also confronted with demands to spend more time with their families. Or they may feel that their

personal values are at odds with those of the company. Or perhaps they feel that their current position is preventing them from pursuing a preferred career path.

5. *People*. Changes in the management structure have increased the number and variety of people that the typical manager confronts every day.

6. *Complexity*. Business organizations and the corporate environment have become increasingly complicated. Planning and execution of operations have become more difficult. Managers can lose direct control over their own accomplishments.

7. *Change*. All businesses are changing more rapidly than in the past. Obsolescence, the need to learn new skills, having to discard familiar routines, accepting new rules and values, are all part of everyday change.

ANXIETY IN ACTION

Sören Kierkegaard, the noted Danish philosopher, devoted considerable study to anxiety in modern life. He compared anxiety to a bridge, the link between possibility and actuality, between plan and action. Only by crossing this bridge could an individual be effective in the world.

As a manager, your goal should be to control and use anxiety, not to avoid it. Consider a common problem of professional actors. No matter how competent and experienced, most actors have to deal with stage fright. This emotion is not really a fear. The actors are not actually afraid of any particular occurrence. Stage fright is a form of anxiety. As the time of the performance approaches, the actors' anxiety builds. They pace, become tense, may even tremble.

While no actor will maintain that this experience is a pleasant one, neither will most actors wish it away. In fact, it is this very anxiety, this painful heightening of senses and feelings, that gives vitality to some actors' performances. Without it, their acting may be ordinary and lifeless.

You have probably experienced a form of stage fright while you waited to give a speech, conducted an important meeting, or opened negotiations with a new client. The sense of anticipation, the uneasiness over something you cannot pinpoint, the inner tension—all make you more aware, help you to concentrate and to summon your total energies to the task.

This is the adaptive function of anxiety. As a manager, you can increase your productivity considerably if you learn to accept this type of anxiety, to control it rather than hide from it, to turn it into a bridge of action rather than let it paralyze you.

ANXIETY AS A SPUR TO ACTION

Energy is vital in business. You have to finish an important report by a certain date. You are responsible for the turn-around of a foundering division. You must effectively handle a seasonal rush of business. In each case, you are likely to experience anxiety. And if you control your anxiety, it can spur you to achievement. Anxiety increases curiosity and makes you more alert. It forces you to confront the future, to look ahead, to form contingency plans. All of these qualities are very useful when facing a novel situation.

Anything new arouses some anxiety because you are

not sure what to expect. You may not fear a specific event, but you prepare yourself, with the help of anxiety, for any possibility. This also makes anxiety useful during a crisis in which you are likely to encounter unfamiliar situations and the need to mobilize energy quickly. Anxiety sometimes arises when you have to make a choice. The manager who has the power to choose a course of action must expect and welcome anxiety.

NEGATIVE REACTIONS TO ANXIETY

While anxiety in moderation can be very beneficial, in excess it can be harmful. Excessive anxiety can lower your resistance to disease, interfere with your sleep, prompt overeating or heavy smoking, and cause heart problems and ulcers. In the end, instead of increasing your productivity, it can damage your effectiveness, prevent you from reaching your goals, and impinge on your emotional comfort.

Anxiety can provide energy for useful work. But some individuals respond to anxiety by engaging in compulsive activity. Compulsive work is usually harmful for two reasons. First, it is rarely goal-oriented or efficient. You expend too much energy on trivial tasks and ignore important ones. You exhaust your energy without really accomplishing much. Second, it does not address the real basis of your anxiety. In order to avoid trying to escape your anxiety through compulsive work:

- Regularly review your work goals and analyze exactly how your current activity is moving you toward those goals.

- Avoid putting off important decisions.

- Examine your priorities. Make sure you are directing your attention to high-priority items first.

- Analyze your daily work load. Could any of your regular tasks readily be delegated to a subordinate?

A little anxiety is not a problem. It becomes a problem when it becomes *pervasive*, when it begins to control your life. Since it has no clear focus, anxiety can spill over from one part of your work to another, and then from your work to the rest of your life. You may thus suffer a continuous low-level anxiety. There are two ways of preventing this ill effect. First, define specific areas of anxiety in writing. For example, you might each week make a list of potentially anxiety-causing responsibilities. Suppose you are planning a new product launching in two months; a new supervisor you've hired has yet to prove his abilities; there is a possible economic recession brewing; and your competitor is preparing a new sales campaign. Feeling anxious about any of these genuine sources is completely normal. But when you do feel the anxiety, recognize its source. Your list will help you to keep the anxiety from spreading to other areas of your work life. Second, use your anxiety as a cue. Once you have pinned down the sources of an anxious feeling, ask, "Is there something I should do about this matter, now?" Perhaps you have overlooked a necessary precaution. Maybe you should have other contingency plans. If so, let your anxiety energize you to complete the task.

Some managers react to anxiety by denying its existence. They ignore genuine sources of anxiety by means of wishful thinking, by selective listening, or by blocking out unpleasant facts. Others respond with near panic. They make impulsive decisions and engage in acting for the sake of action, with little regard for consequences. Still others try to share what is really their own responsibility. They attempt to shift the blame to colleagues and subordinates. Be aware of all these negative responses to an anxiety-producing situation.

POSITIVE REACTIONS TO ANXIETY

In order to get the most benefit out of the anxiety you experience on the job, try any of these four techniques:

1. *Action.* Attack the source of your anxiety directly. Put it to work immediately. For example, if a difficult analysis is bothering you, set to work on it immediately. You'll find that even a short period of actual activity will greatly reduce your anxiety. The more successfully you can turn the energy of anxiety into goal-oriented actions, the more the emotion will help you. One problem that managers encounter in this regard is a rigidity in their routines. Try to introduce more flexibility into your schedule. This will allow you to make better use of the energy provided by anxiety. For example, if you are anxious about a speech you have to give, take some time to go over it now, even though you normally reserve this time of day for meeting with subordinates. If you feel anxious about next year's budget, take the figures home with you and go over them at night, even though that is not your usual habit.

2. *Relaxation.* Deliberate relaxation is one way to prevent anxiety from spreading into other areas of your life. This may consist of anything from a series of short breaks in your schedule to a formal program of meditation or exercise. Simple calisthenics or jogging have proven very beneficial for keeping anxiety within limits.

You might find it helpful to take an occasional short walk—keeping your mind on what you are doing rather than dwelling on the source of your anxiety. Means of relaxation are discussed in later chapters.

3. *Analysis*. Uncertainty and confusion are sources of inordinate anxiety. The more you clarify your view of work, the less anxiety you will experience. Whenever you feel a general uneasiness, take time to ask yourself the following questions. Answer clearly, preferably in writing:

- What are my short-term goals?

- How do these goals fit in with my long-term career plans?

- What are my most important assets and talents?

- Am I using them in the best way to reach my goals?

- What liabilities or weaknesses should I watch out for?

- Which are the most important opportunities facing me now?

- Which problems before me are the most difficult?

- Am I experiencing any conflict between my work duties and my responsibilities to my family or to myself?

- How does the way my company is organized help or hinder me in my attempt to reach my goals?

4. *Planning*. Planning is the most effective way to avoid excessive anxiety. In many instances, anxiety occurs because you have not planned carefully enough. Too many uncertainties remain. You have left yourself exposed to risk.

Planning, of course, does not eliminate risk entirely, but it does allow you to calculate your risks. For example, the risk of failure does not keep you from launching a new product. But because there is an element of risk in introducing any new product, you carefully consider your investment in raw materials and inventory, your expenditures on marketing, and your alteration of plans. Perhaps you form contingency marketing plans if the primary campaign does not yield sufficient sales. Or you decide in advance at what point to abandon the project if it proves unprofitable. All this planning is spurred by anxiety over the success of the product. The plans themselves keep your anxiety under control because they reduce your apprehension over negative uncertainties.

When you are planning, however, you must avoid inflexibility. Sometimes managers go too far in trying to control anxiety. They paralyze themselves with rigid plans that make too few allowances for unpredictable events and spontaneous actions.

STRESS: FRIEND OR FOE?

Recently, a great deal of attention has been paid to managerial stress: its sources, its effects, how to handle it. Stress is a nonspecific response of the body to any demand made on it. This response often includes anxiety. Stress is not a negative factor. It cannot be avoided. A study conducted by the American Management Associations recently found that a majority of managers viewed stress as an opportunity rather than an obstacle. You'll be reading about managerial stress in detail in the next section.

ANSWERS:
HOW WOULD YOU HANDLE IT?

1. The best answer is *b*. Ann Lanson's anxiety stems largely from uncertainty about the course of her career. She is not sure which way she wants to proceed or whether she is qualified for her current career path. A review of her goals would clarify her future and show her any weaknesses that she should rectify. She could then address specific rather than vague problems.

   Taking more vacations will not help her as long as this uncertainty remains. A transfer to a lower position is a possibility. But to take that way out immediately is to back down from her responsibility. The chances are that she can achieve her goals once she clarifies them. Simply telling herself to stop worrying will have little effect on this potent problem.

2. The best answer is *d*. Relaxed time constraints, group identity, and emotonal outlets are all valuable antidotes to the kind of burnout that is affecting this department.

9

ADDRESSING
THE NEGATIVE ASPECTS
OF DEPRESSION

All forms of depression are related to one another. Simple sadness, for example, is the mildest form of depression and can grow into a more serious condition.

The forms of depression are frequently divided into three categories:

Sadness.   The unhappy feeling you have about a particular event is known as sadness—the discouragement you feel, for example, when an important customer you've been trying to attract refuses to buy from your company. Or sadness may be a melancholy mood with no apparent cause. Sadness is always transient, usually lasting only a few hours or a day or two. It is unaccompanied by any distortions in thinking.

Acute depression.   This type of depression is caused by a specific instigating event, has very clear-cut symptoms, and is not permanent. It can be mild and short-lived, or it can be very intense and long-lasting—the prolonged grief you feel after the death of a family member or colleague, for instance. It differs from mere sadness in that it can distort your perspective. You may see the future as totally bleak when in fact, considered objectively, it holds the potential for renewed happiness. You may even feel that you are no longer capable of functioning effectively. Sometimes acute depression, when it continues for an excessive length of time, can grow into chronic depression.

Chronic depression. This degree of depression is not directly connected with an initiating circumstance. It may develop very gradually so that you cannot say exactly when it began. It involves the same distorted perspective as acute depression, but it may last much longer. Chronic depression is a form of stress that wears you down, deepening your despondency.

DEPRESSION: AN OCCUPATIONAL HAZARD

As a manager you are particularly vulnerable to depression. In fact, depression is sometimes referred to as the "emotion of achievement." Two primary factors make managers susceptible to depression. The first is stress. Depression can result from an excess of tension and pressure on the job. You expend too much psychological energy trying to handle the demands of your work, and you may reach a state of mental exhaustion. Depression then serves as a retreat from stress, a regenerative period forced on you by your own system. Second, the achievement that every manager experiences can itself touch off depression. You are no longer engaged in a struggle to win promotion and recognition, as you were when you were younger. Perhaps the rewards of the position you have attained are disappointing. Or you feel that you've paid too high a price in order to achieve your ambition. Either of these situations can give rise to depression.

LOCATING THE CAUSE OF DEPRESSION

The most direct instigator of depression is an *overt loss*. This can occur when a loved one dies. The grief you feel is usually a temporary emotion. Bereavement, however, can produce more intense acute depression, particularly if you have lost someone with whom you had a deep emotional involvement.

Any loss can result in depression. You lose an important business opportunity. You apply for a new position and fail to be appointed. You find that you have been betrayed by someone you trusted. You lose faith in that person.

Relocation is another common source of depression for the manager. Moving to a new city means the loss of close contacts with old friends, the loss of a familiar environment and pattern of living. Or depression can be brought on by a circumstance that diminishes your self-esteem. Illness, for example, often results in depression. The urgent need to learn a new job skill or a sudden increase in your responsibilities can also instigate depression. Since any learning experience can result in mistakes, which undermine your confidence, new demands on the job frequently lead to depression.

RECOGNIZING THE SYMPTOMS OF DEPRESSION

You can take certain precautions to avoid the harmful effects of depression in yourself and your associates. The first step is to recognize and deal with it.

Many managers deny the existence of their depression. They attribute its symptoms to stress or physical ailments or fatigue. They may try to chase away their depression with an intensified work pace or cover it up with false cheerfulness. Meanwhile, the longer they refuse to face their real feelings, the worse the depression becomes.

In order to recognize symptoms of depression in yourself and others, go through the checklist in Exhibit 12. If you are experiencing a number of these symptoms, ask yourself why. Have there been any major losses in your life in the recent past? Have you experienced significant changes of any kind? Have any events threatened or diminished your self-esteem? Are you undergoing any unusual stress?

POSITIVE ASPECTS OF DEPRESSION

Once you have learned to recognize mild depression, you can attempt to turn it to your benefit. Depression is often the *first warning sign* that you are experiencing more stress than you can manage. Recognizing your depression will allow you to deal with the stress before it creates more serious problems for you.

Depression can serve as a coping mechanism. As a manager, you are often expected to suppress your emotional reactions to the stress and tensions associated with your job.

EXHIBIT 12

Symptoms of Depression

Here are some common symptoms of depression. This list is designed only as a set of guidelines, not as a definitive test for depression. We all experience depression in slightly different ways, with our own group of symptoms. This list may be useful in helping you, a subordinate, or a colleague to recognize depression.

- Constant sleep disturbance such as inability to fall asleep or early waking.

- Aches and pains that have no physical source.

- Frequent headaches or a feeling of pressure in the head.

- A feeling that you will ultimately fail in life.

- Compulsive work, especially with few concrete achievements; any other compulsive behavior, such as overeating.

- A feeling that you have few alternatives to your present view of your life and work.

- Social isolation: the desire to cut off social ties and be alone; a feeling of alienation from others.

- A feeling that you are totally out of control of the events of your life, that you are being swept along by fate.

- Difficulty concentrating or remembering.

- Increased use of alcohol, sedatives, stimulants, or other drugs.

- A feeling of inner emptiness.

- A feeling that life has no value or purpose.

- Loneliness, a sense of having no one to confide in.

- Reduced interest in your work or the world in general.

- A feeling that you lack the ability to handle your responsibilities.

- Excessive procrastination about simple decisions and tasks.

- Relinquishing your goals or viewing them as unimportant.

- Frequent negative thoughts about yourself.

You are encouraged to continue to function even though you may be in a state of inner turmoil.

The experiences that cause depression—loss, frustration, prolonged stress—also drain you of your psychological energy. Your psychological liabilities—the need to handle change and challenge—overwhelm your assets—strength and resilience.

A mild depression represents a natural means of equalizing your emotional balance sheet. It is a time of reduced activity, of conservation and renewal of psychological energy. Depression also can provide you with an opportunity to break frustrating and ineffective patterns of behavior. Everyone experiences losses. And every loss requires a psychological reorientation. Depression can serve as an automatic mechanism for accomplishing that reorientation.

The alternative to feeling depressed is to deny your feelings entirely. This may, in the short run, allow you to maintain your routine and continue to produce in your job, but in the long run the consequences will be disastrous. You will become less and less sensitive to your own feelings and less empathetic to those of others. You could become hardened, resistant to spontaneity, and incapable of learning anything new.

HOW TO HANDLE DEPRESSION

If you think you are suffering from a mild case of depression, or heading in that direction, you can take these seven steps to counteract your state.

1. *Accept the depression.* Do not try to deny it through forced cheerfulness or continuous activity, or to escape it by traveling or using alcohol. Generally, experts agree that any sad or despondent mood that continues for two weeks or longer is a sign of true depression. But remember that depression can also be masked.

2. *Review the causes of your depression.* Accept the fact that you have a right to feel sad and disappointed over the loss of an opportunity or a friend. Evaluate the importance of the loss. Give yourself a period of time to adjust to the loss.

3. *Examine your feelings.* Once you have pinpointed the cause of your depression, consider exactly what it is you feel. Focusing on your feelings brings depression out into the open, and is the first step toward both alleviating it and using it to your benefit. In order to view your feelings more objectively, you may find it helpful to write them down. Make a list of the problems that are troubling you. Analyze how you feel about them and about yourself.

4. *Relax.* If your depression is accompanied by fatigue, a few days away from work may help to restore the energy you need to revitalize yourself. Time to relax will also

prevent you from engaging in the excessive work that frequently masks depression. Don't take a long vacation, though, because inactivity and boredom can contribute to depression.

5. *Communicate with others.* Isolation contributes to the escalation of depression. As you become more depressed, you feel less and less like talking with your friends. This social isolation, though, tends to increase depression. You become lonely and have no one to counter your own distorted view of yourself. Get in touch with close friends whenever you feel depressed. Maintain your social life, even if at a less ambitious pace than normal. Don't shut yourself off from other people because you are afraid of depressing them.

6. *Rebuild your self-esteem.* When you are depressed, you magnify your mistakes and shortcomings and undervalue your strengths and achievements. This leads directly to an increase in your depression: the lower your self-esteem, the worse you feel. Instead of giving in to it, *use* your depression as an opportunity for self-evaluation. Begin concretely by analyzing your achievements and strengths. Review specific instances in which you've accomplished your goals. Think of processes you've used to solve difficult problems. List the ways in which you've helped other managers. It is also useful to write down your negative feelings about yourself. Depression feeds on self-criticism. When you write your thoughts down, you can more easily see them as the distortions they probably are.

7. *Become active.* Once you have recognized and dealt with the basis of your depression, the best way to get yourself out of it is to become active. If you give in to the lethargy that accompanies depression—sitting alone for long periods and shunning activity, for example—

you are creating the kind of environment that prolongs depression. If you force yourself to become involved in tasks or recreational activities that you enjoy, you will more quickly arise from your depression. Avoid high-pressure work assignments when you are depressed, however. Instead, look for tasks you can readily accomplish and in which you will see concrete results quickly. Sports, moderate exercise, and other recreational activities can be very helpful in alleviating depression and helping you to regenerate your emotional stability.

FOUR WAYS TO PREVENT SEVERE DEPRESSION

Almost all managers can expect to experience some degree of depression occasionally, but you can take important steps to avoid serious depression.

Channel your hostility. Depression can result from the stress caused by suppressed or inappropriately expressed hostility. Managers are particularly susceptible to this type of depression because they must regularly confront subordinates, colleagues, customers, and others. Review Chapter 2, "Using Anger as an Effective Tool in Business," and study ways of channeling your hostility so that it does not work to your disadvantage.

Avoid a depressing environment. To whatever extent possible within the structure of your job and company, try to create an environment that includes these elements:

• Frequent interaction with colleagues

- Variety in both type and pace of work
- Clear assignments and unambiguous lines of authority
- Acceptance of emotional expression and shared feelings
- Open lines of communication at all levels
- Official recognition of even small accomplishments

Express your feelings. Work toward becoming more emotionally expressive. If you find that difficult, look for someone with whom you can openly discuss how you feel—a colleague, perhaps, or your clergyman or physician. This safety valve can be very beneficial in keeping unacknowledged feelings from causing or adding to depression.

Learn to cope with stress. All managers face stress on the job. If you do not confront and cope with stress, your system will eventually rebel, and depression may be the result. To combat stress:

- Avoid procrastinating
- Organize your work in a clear and effective manner
- Delegate authority efficiently
- Set specific and realistic goals
- Take a group approach to problems rather than handling them alone

ADVISING A DEPRESSED ASSOCIATE

Depression can become a severe emotional disturbance. Colleagues who are seriously depressed may be unable to cope with their feelings alone. Psychotherapy can be useful for resolving even mild depression. The following four conditions might prompt you to recommend that an associate consider seeking professional help:

Prolonged depression. Even severe depression should begin to diminish spontaneously after two weeks. If it does not, or if it seems to be growing more intense, recommend professional treatment.

Disruption of daily life. Depression can reduce the energy and efficiency with which your colleagues go about their daily tasks. If you see that depression seems to be totally disrupting their normal routine, you may want to suggest that they seek therapy.

Escape. If any colleague is seeking escape in alcohol or drug abuse, you should consider depression as a possible underlying cause. The misuse of sleeping pills or stimulants, for instance, is often a sign that the depressed person needs help.

Despondency. The most serious danger of depression is suicide. The intense sadness and despair of depression can sometimes lead directly to thoughts of self-destruction. If you suspect that a colleague is considering suicide, you should urgently recommend immediate treatment.

Here are some other tactics for dealing with depressed associates:

- *Empathize.* Identify with your colleagues' feelings of despondency and hopelessness. They cannot be easily cheered up or reasoned out of their mood. Let them know that you understand their feelings and consider them normal.

- *Advise them to avoid isolation.* Being alone tends to worsen depression. Even though your colleagues may resist interacting with their co-workers, try to get them involved in a task force or committee.

- *Relieving stress.* Don't expect depressed colleagues to function at 100 percent of their capacity. Extend their deadlines and make sure they realize that there is no pressure on them.

- *Get them involved.* While you should not put too much stress on them, neither should you remove their opportunity to do productive work. Short-term assignments that you know are within their capacity are useful to help them rebuild their self-esteem and remain active.

PART II

CONTROLLING STRESS

INTRODUCTION

Stress can be extremely debilitating for managers. Headaches, ulcers, hypertension, and nervous disorders can be linked directly to too much stress in the managerial lifestyle.

However, it's within the power of most individuals to cope with and ultimately conquer stress. Properly handled, its deleterious effects can be minimized. But accomplishing this means acquiring a precise understanding of the nature of stress and what it does to you during the course of a workday. You must be able to recognize the early warning signs that your body and mind give off, and you must be willing take action before stress overcomes you.

The analysis and guidelines that follow explain the causes, prevention, and treatment of stress. You'll learn not only how to handle personal stress but also how to spot it and deal with it in your colleagues and subordinates. In essence, stress is handled best by those who understand it. Here's your first step on your way to the mastering of stress.

WHAT IS STRESS?

We can't avoid stress. We encounter stressful stimuli (stressors) many times a day. Even when we sleep, we can have stressful dreams. Stress is essential to daily living. It's the driving, constructive force behind creativity and achievement in business, science, the arts, sports, and every other field of endeavor.

STRESS CAN BE PLEASANT OR UNPLEASANT

Stress can be extremely pleasant and exciting when it's induced by a business triumph, a great athletic victory, marriage, the birth of a child, or similar happy events. Business lunches, conferences, and meetings with interesting people present pleasurable but lesser stresses. Even a game of chess or golf can be stressful. Pleasant stresses are not harmful unless they are piled one upon another in rapid succession.

Stress can be extremely unpleasant and destructive, however, when it's caused by fear, severe physical over-exertion, humiliating censure, disastrous business losses, physical injury, the death of a loved one. These extreme stresses usually cause the body to react more severely.

The late Hans Selye, long considered the world's leading authority on stress, defined stress as "the nonspecific response of the body to any demand upon it." The body makes different responses to different stimuli, such as heat, cold, pain, loss of blood, or joyful, sorrowful, or frightening experiences. If the demands on the body are excessive, Dr. Selye called the result *distress*.

The body's responses vary according to how the individual perceives the sources of stress. For example, the shock of unexpectedly losing a customer who accounts for a major share of the business would cause in a manager an emotional reaction quite different from the elation that results from a sudden decision by the same customer to double his orders. Yet, in either of these instances, the body undergoes similar glandular responses and physiological changes. It's immaterial what kind of experience starts them in motion. The glands release large quantities of adrenaline, cortisone, and other hormones to produce physiological changes in the body: heartbeat and breathing speed up; blood vessels dilate.

HOW PEOPLE RESPOND TO STRESS

In primitive times, stress reactions served a useful purpose. When cave dwellers heard a noise that frightened them, their body chemistry was mobilized so that they could defend themselves. They reacted by hurling stones or by running away.

Today's business managers encounter stimuli that are much more complex than those faced by primitive people. They can't run away or throw things, however. Often, they can't even display fear or rage. They must hide their intense emotional reactions. And repressing emotions can have adverse physiological and psychological consequences.

When stressors involve relations with other people, another response (besides fighting or fleeing) is possible: adapting to the stress. In many cases, people recover from the immediate effects of a stressful experience rather quickly. They have a good supply of superficial adaptation energy to use and replenish as necessary, like money in a checking account. Nevertheless, stress does take a toll. When energy reserves are depleted it's most difficult to replenish them.

Managers can squander their adaptation energy recklessly, or they can make this valuable resource last longer by using it wisely and sparingly, only when the stress encountered in an activity is worthwhile. This requires that they understand what stress is, learn their individual capacities to cope with or adapt to it, and find out what levels of stress they can tolerate. If they know more about the effects of stress, they are more likely to regulate their exposure to stressful situations.

The Holmes Stress Scale

No simple rule of thumb can measure precisely how much stress is too much, but Thomas Holmes, professor of psychiatry at the University of Washington, has developed a point system that evaluates stressors often encountered in business and personal life. Dr. Holmes's research indicates that experiencing 300 points of stress during one year is dangerous for a typical adult. Some 80 percent of the people he studied who exceeded 300 points became depressed or suffered serious physical illnesses. He assigned the following point values to both pleasant and unpleasant occurrences:

Death of a spouse	100
Marital separation	65
Death of a close family member	63
Personal injury or illness	53
Marriage	50
Loss of job	47
Marital reconciliation	45
Retirement	45
Change in health of a family member	44
Wife's pregnancy	40
Sex difficulties	39
Gain of a new family member	39
Change in financial status	38
Death of a close friend	37
Change to a different kind of work	36
Increase or decrease in arguments with spouse	35
Taking out a big mortgage on home	31
Foreclosure of mortgage or loan	30
Change in work responsibilities	29
Son or daughter leaving home	29
Trouble with in-laws	29
Outstanding personal achievement	28

Spouse beginning or stopping work	29
Revision of personal habits	24
Trouble with business superior	23
Change in work hours or conditions	20
Change of residence	20
Change of schools	20
Change in type of recreation	19
Change in frequency or nature of social activities	18
Taking out a small mortgage on home	17
Change in sleeping habits	16
Change in number of family get-togethers	15
Change in eating habits	15
Vacation	13
Minor violations of law	11

Now that we have defined stress and seen that stressors individually or in combination can affect a person's health, let's take a closer look at the stress mechanism itself.

General Adaptation Syndrome

Suppose that you're driving your car, approaching a stop light at an intersection, when another car suddenly swerves in front of you. You slam on your brakes and turn sharply to avoid a collision as the other car screeches to a halt. You jump out of your car, march over to the other driver, and give him a thorough scolding. You've responded to this highly stressful situation with intense fear, followed by blazing anger. These two emotions trigger physiological changes that conform exactly to the first two stages in the three-state theory of stress developed by Dr. Selye. His theory (which he calls the General Adaptation Syndrome or G.A.S.) is the cornerstone of modern research on stress. The stages are:

1. *Alarm reaction.* On first exposure to the stressor, the body tries to avoid or contain this stimulus by strengthening itself with hormones and with coordinated changes in the central nervous system. This is a dangerous phase when the body's resistance is diminished.

2. *Resistance stage.* Bodily signs of the alarm reaction virtually disappear. If exposure to the stressor continues and the body can adapt to it, resistance ensues and rises above normal. Specific bodily reactions occur to contain effects of the stressor. In an injury, for instance, white blood corpuscles rush to the site.

3. *Exhaustion state.* After long exposure to stress, eventually adaptation energy becomes exhausted. Harmful reactions spread throughout the body.

EFFECTS OF STRESS

Dr. Selye emphasized in his writings that, although prolonged severe stress can cause emotional depression, the exhaustion stage is not depression, but a physical process.

Long-lasting excessive stress can cause a variety of physical illnesses as well as depression. Among them: high blood pressure, ulcers, colitis, arthritis, diabetes, stroke, and heart attack. The same type and level of stress affects different people differently. Whether the heart, kidneys, gastrointestinal tract, or psychological well-being will suffer most may depend on the person's physical condition (for example, genetic predisposition, age, and sex) and on certain external factors (diet, or treatment with certain drugs or hormones). The weakest link in a chain breaks down under stress, even though all parts are equally exposed to it.

But people also require a certain amount of stress to be happy. Many people suffer as much from purposeless existence as from excessive striving. Of course, there are great differences in the amount of stress a person needs for happiness.

HOW TO IDENTIFY A STRESS DISORDER

Stress disorders usually develop slowly, without the victim being clearly aware of what is happening. The list of stages below can help you measure your own reactions to stress and advise your fellow managers when you suspect that they are under excessive stress.

The symptoms of a stress disorder are frequently conflicting and confusing. Some people will have some of the symptoms, and other people will have others. At each stage, symptoms usually get worse. Sometimes, however, certain symptoms will lessen or disappear, and others take their place. These guidelines were developed by Robert J. Van Amberg, a practicing psychiatrist in Montclair, New Jersey.

Six Stages of Stress

Stage I.   This is a mild stress stage usually accompanied by the following:

1. Great zest

2. Unusually acute perception

3. Excessive nervous energy and ability to accomplish more work than usual

This stage is so pleasant that many people become almost addicted to it. They want to maintain it. Unfortunately, it must be considered an early warning sign that energy reserves are being drawn down.

Stage II.   At this stage, some of the unpleasant effects of stress appear. Energy reserves no longer last through the day. These symptoms are common:

1. Tiredness after rising, or flagging energy after lunch or early in the afternoon

2. Occasional disturbance of bowel and stomach functions, heart flutters

3. Tightness of muscles in the back and around the skull

4. A feeling of being unable to relax

Stage III.   At this stage, tiredness becomes more pronounced. Other symptoms include:

1. Greater disturbances of bowel functions

2. Stomach trouble

3. Muscle tightening

4. Increased feelings of tenseness

5. Sleep disturbances

6. Faintness

At this point, a visit to a doctor is advisable. Unless demands are reduced and the body is allowed to recover its energy supply, more serious problems will arise in the later stages.

Stage IV.   At this stage the following symptoms may occur:

1. Great difficulty in getting through the day

2. Once-pleasant activities are now quite difficult

3. Loss of ability to respond to social affairs, conversations with friends, and other activities, which now seem burdensome

4. Greater disturbance of sleep—unpleasant dreams, for example, or awakening between 3:00 and 5:30 in the morning

5. A feeling of negativism

6. Inability to concentrate

7. Nameless fears

Stage V.   This stage is represented by a deepening of the symptoms:

1. Extreme fatigue

2. Difficulty in managing fairly simple tasks

3. Extreme disturbances of bowel and stomach functions

4. Pervasive fear

Stage VI.   This is the final stage and can produce terrifying symptoms:

1. Heart pounding and panic caused by release of adrenaline

2. Gasping for breath

3. Trembling, shivering, sweating

4. Numb and tingling hands and feet

5. Sheer exhaustion, barely enough energy to do even the most simple tasks

The stress disorder is essentially a step-by-step exhaustion of the body's fuel reserves. In some people, the principal symptom is tiredness; in others, the main symptom is anxiety or depression.

Anxiety is characterized by tension and exaggerated fears. This state is caused by a speeding up of bodily processes resulting in a steady exhaustion of body fuel. During the latter stages of exhaustion, the victim may be depressed. This stage is caused by a slowdown of bodily processes as a result of exhaustion.

Symptoms of Anxiety

The early warning signals of anxiety are often physiological. They include:

- Rapid pulse (including consciousness of heartbeat)

- Excessive perspiration

- Frequent urination

- Diarrhea or constipation (although constipation is more likely to be a sign of depression than of anxiety)

- High blood pressure

- A feeling of tension

A routine physical can detect some of the physiological symptoms, but often the doctor will simply tell the patient that there is nothing essentially wrong. In other words, the doctor cannot diagnose a physical illness. Nevertheless, it is most important that the manager under stress have frequent physical checkups.

Besides physical symptoms, anxiety triggers psychological symptoms that are revealed in a person's living and working habits. Exaggerated fear is one symptom. Insomnia is another important signal. The anxious manager may frequently wake up in the middle of the night for no apparent reason and then be unable to fall back to sleep.

John F. O'Connor, associate professor of clinical psychology at the Columbia University College of Physicians and Surgeons, points out that insomnia is a problem in both anxiety and depression, but with a significant difference. The anxious person can't sleep because of tension and nerves. Tossing and turning are common. However, the depressed person's sleeplessness tends to be quiet, mournful, and listless.

Sudden Changes That May Signal Anxiety

Dr. O'Connor, who is also a psychiatric consultant to several leading corporations, emphasizes that any sudden, significant, unexplained change in a manager's personal or professional behavior can serve as an indication to others that the person is under excessive stress. Here are some examples manifested by managers suffering from anxiety:

- Sudden heavy drinking or smoking
- A change in sex habits, an increase or decrease in frequency of sexual activity—although loss of sex drive is more likely a symptom of depression than of anxiety

- Sudden difficulty making decisions, a tendency to make the safest rather than the best choice

- The onset of frequent irritability

- Excessive activity, suddenly working late at the office several nights a week

- Sudden gain or loss in weight

- Going on a diet or adopting a health fad

- Escaping responsibilities

- Changing moral standards, cutting ethical corners

- Overreacting to minor problems

- Making mistakes and forgetting things

In severe cases of anxiety, such symptoms become more pronounced and numerous. They are usually the main evidence that a manager needs to take definite steps to deal with a stress problem.

STRESS-INDUCED ACTIVITY CHANGES

Stress can have a complex impact on a company. For example, a manager of a major television corporation sought Dr. O'Connor's help in facing a highly stressful conflict between himself and his superior. All this coincided with a significant deterioration in the superior's personal and professional behavior, also undoubtedly due to the stress he was under. He ran up big bills for lavish entertainment of business contacts. He started to drink heavily and often appeared drunk. And he had an indiscreet love affair.

With Dr. O'Connor's help, his client weathered the conflict with his boss until he found a new position with another large TV company at a much higher level and larger salary than his former superior, who still has his job, but has been repeatedly passed over for promotion.

Another case involved a marketing manager for a large international electronics firm to which the Industrial Service Division of the Psychological Corporation, in New York, is a consultant. This manager suddenly began to avoid her responsibilities on a major scale. She manufactured a reason for taking an unnecessary trip as a technical representative on a company project. Immediately afterward, she took an unscheduled vacation. Then she took more time off for a management development seminar. Her company was on the brink of firing her. But Frederick C. Rockett, the Psychological Corporation's expert on stress, recognized the manager's behavior patterns as a sign of heavy stress and advised treatment. The manager followed this advice and kept her job.

Psychological Consulting Services

As these examples show, managers may not recognize or even want to recognize that they have a serious stress problem. Someone else may have to bring it to their attention— a friend, perhaps, or business associate, superior, spouse, doctor, or professional consultant.

But too often the people closest to the managers—those who see the symptoms—don't realize the nature of the problem or won't mention it. Then, if the troubled managers continue their unusual behavior, their jobs may be in jeopardy.

That's why many companies now hire psychological consultants. From their objective vantage point, consultants often recognize problems that aren't apparent to managers within the company. Also, since consultants aren't directly linked to the company, they can be much more frank than an insider in pointing out problems.

CAUSES AND SYMPTOMS OF DEPRESSION

Dr. Tobias Brocher, a psychiatrist and director of the Menninger Foundation's Center for Applied Behavioral Science, says that tests show that depression is one of the most prevalent and serious problems for managers.

"A high percentage of managers suffer from depression, although it's often hidden," he explained. "It's usually related to stress. When a manager becomes angry or anxious, often he can't vent his feelings or find legitimate outlets for his aggressions. He may not even admit them to himself. So he becomes depressed as a defense against feelings he doesn't want to recognize in himself."

Dr. O'Connor points out that depression is often caused by the loss of something or someone a manager values highly or by a significant defeat in business, the death of a loved one or a close friend, or marital trouble.

But, the psychiatrist added, depression can also be caused by prolonged exposure to less severe stress or an accumulation of stresses and pressures on the job.

The causes of depression are often subtle, according to Daniel J. Levinson, a leading psychiatrist at Yale University. He notes that managers often become deeply depressed when their careers reach a plateau at middle age, and they realize their chances for further promotion are limited. This period is sometimes called the middle-age crisis.

Managers also may become deeply depressed in their fifties and early sixties when they approach retirement or after they actually do retire. If they haven't developed other interests, they feel they are no longer useful or have no reason for living.

SIGNS OF DEPRESSION

When people are depressed, they may not look depressed or even realize that they're depressed. The symptoms may be quite subtle and some resemble the symptoms of severe anxiety. Among them:

- Listlessness
- Withdrawal or lack of interest in events
- Irritability
- Constipation
- Insomnia (the mournful type)
- Excessive sleeping
- Frequent daydreaming
- Tearfulness
- Terrifying dreams
- Heavy drinking
- Use of drugs
- Loss of sex drive
- Slowness in making decisions
- Thoughts of one's own worthlessness
- Feelings of rejection

- Thoughts of suicide

- Attempts at suicide

In a severe case, a depressed individual may just stay in bed all day and watch television, sleep, or stare at the wall. Nothing provides pleasure. Such an individual definitely needs professional treatment. Depression is less likely than anxiety to lead to psychosomatic illness, but it can do so.

As with anxiety, any sudden change in a manager's performance or living patterns may be a danger signal— for instance, if the manager is quite neat, but suddenly turns sloppy. A sudden reduction in sex life, for no apparent reason, is often a signal. Suddenly shirking responsibilities or taking excessive time off from work may be a symptom of depression.

A reasonable amount of depression is natural following a death or some other deep loss. But normally its impact lessens with the passage of time. If the symptoms continue for more than a few weeks, or at worst a month or two, the person undoubtedly needs professional help.

IS STRESS A MENTAL ILLNESS?

The symptoms of stress disorders are so bewildering that managers may doubt their own mental stability. Excessive fears—such as the fear of walking on the street, going to church, or even going to a store—may well lead them to question their sanity. They may also be unable to concentrate, and their behavior in social and business situations may be quite inappropriate.

Despite these symptoms, most managers suffering from stress disorders are not mentally ill. Such individuals have a good grasp on reality, and they certainly will do no harm to others. In fact, managers suffering from stress are frequently quite thoughtful of others and tend to go out of their way to be pleasant. People who are in an anxiety state often take great care not to provoke any kind of adverse emotional reactions in those around them. In a depressed state, they operate at such a low level of activity that it would be difficult for them to summon up the required energy reserves to antagonize their colleagues.

As the symptoms of a stress disorder pass, the psychological state improves correspondingly. When the manager is well again, he or she usually has a far greater knowledge of the interactions of the body and the mind. In fact, managers who have passed through severe stress disorders may wind up being emotionally healthier than their contemporaries.

True mental illnesses such as manic depression, paranoia, and schizophrenia result in more bizarre behavior than anything found in a stress disorder. Severe mental illness affects only a small percentage of the population.

CAUSES OF
STRESS AMONG MANAGERS

Most managers are exposed to quite similar stressful stimuli. But the same stressor that causes one person mild exhilaration can cause someone else deep anxiety. This difference in reaction depends on how the person perceives the problem that causes stress. If one thinks one can cope with it, self-esteem is reinforced. If an individual thinks he or she cannot cope, loss of self-esteem results.

STRESSORS COMMON
TO MOST MANAGERS

Changes are a fundamental source of stress to you as a manager. Each time you receive a major promotion to a new position, you lose the psychological guideposts to which you have become accustomed, and you must adapt to new ones. A new, larger, fancier office is a pleasant stimulus. But it also presents a stressful challenge for you to succeed in your new responsibilities.

Big changes in your work routines are stressful, often mildly and pleasantly, but sometimes severely. Working with different people can also be stressful. The tools you work with—desk, telephone, intercom, and dictating machine—become part of your environment. To some extent, as a manager, you identify with them. Getting used to new ones is part of adapting to a new position. That's why taking desktop objects from your old office to the new one may help you make the transition. Increasing demands on your time are also stressful. More numerous and more pressing deadlines are stressful. So are increases in traveling and entertaining.

But these factors don't necessarily get worse in higher management. In fact, higher-ranking executives have more control over their own schedules. Chief executives usually completely control their schedules. Travel can be relaxing. The CEO often can arrange trips at convenient times and include several days' vacation. Lower-echelon managers have less control over their work loads. Their travel schedules are governed largely by their company's operations.

STRESSFUL ROLES MANAGERS PLAY

Many managers find their role as mentor to a department or staff uncomfortable. They find the dependence of their subordinates irritating. They may find it stressful to have to measure carefully every word they utter for fear that it might be misinterpreted. Managers must also bear the stress of being criticized by subordinates who don't like their decisions. The managers constantly risk being called unfair or prejudiced—and even being hated.

Decisions that adversely affect other people's lives are particularly stressful. Most managers find it emotionally painful to discharge subordinates or pass them over for promotion. Yet they must take such actions. Then, afterwards, they have the difficult problem of motivating people who have been passed over for promotion but who nevertheless can continue to make valuable contributions to the company.

Constant and routine relationships with difficult people cause stress among managers at all levels. It is particularly hard to adapt to such relationships in changing situations.

Difficult subordinates and customers are the easiest to handle. Frederick C. Rockett, expert on stress at the Psychological Corporation, describes these relationships as "more like a tight-fitting shoe than a knife at the throat." Managers have a good deal of control over subordinates. Dissatisfied customers can usually be pacified, since they benefit as much from the business relationship as the supplier does.

Clashes between a manager and a new boss or between managers of equal rank, however, often cause severe stress, particularly after mergers in which managers of two different companies suddenly are forced to work closely together. Even the chief executive of a company can become involved in stressfull conflicts with antagonistic directors or large stockholders.

Relations with the government are an increasing source of stress among managers. As the government becomes more active in such areas as energy conservation, consumer and environmental protection, its regulation of business gets tougher and more complex.

For example, a large gas and water utility in the northeastern United States was recently under such pressure from government allocators and price regulators that its financial survival was jeopardized. The government's actions put the company's president under severe stress.

Competitive pressures for advancement often cause stress among managers in a company. These pressures become particularly intense among middle-echelon executives. Promotional opportunities suddenly narrow sharply. Individuals become aware that they're unlikely to reach their lofty career goals. They often are beset by fear of failure, fear of being passed over for promotion or even of being fired, fear of making a crucial mistake, fear of being undermined by other managers, fear of retaliation by an unfriendly superior. Such fears are part of the middle-age crisis. They can be pronounced in companies that don't regularly let employees know where they stand and what their future opportunities within the company are.

INNER CONFLICTS AS A CAUSE OF STRESS

Inner emotional conflicts are a devastating source of stress. In severe cases, they can bring on depression. They are often related to other stressors.

The root causes of this kind of stress are usually repressed emotions and thwarted desires. Most managers think they are supposed to conceal their emotions. They may not even reveal their true feelings to themselves. Among their superiors, equals, and subordinates, managers maintain an appearance of calm, confident competence, never showing anger, aggression, or fear. To do so might make them less effective as leaders and ruin their chances of promotion.

Most managers cannot discuss their feelings with anyone else in the company. Competitive pressures are a barrier to deep personal friendships in a business organization. They can't establish close relationships with subordinates, because they must exercise authority over those people and make decisions affecting their careers. Neither can they open up to their superiors for fear of appearing to lack confidence in themselves.

This is particularly a problem for top managers. After they reach the top, their isolation from other people in the organization often becomes absolute. They can't even bare their feelings to their most senior subordinates, and they certainly cannot expect frank opinions or advice from lower-echelon subordinates.

The most serious inner conflicts are felt by managers who aren't psychologically suited to their jobs, which are not what they really prefer to do in life. And they may not even be aware of the psychological misfit. Their dissatisfaction may be entirely subconscious.

A conflict in values and attitudes can cause stress in managers who have been promoted to higher positions. For instance, they may have achieved success in their lower positions in spite of their fairly rigid attitudes or their compulsion always to go strictly by the rules. But the new responsibilities may require them to be much more flexible. To be really successful, they may have to bend or adjust the rules to fit different situations. Adapting to this new way of thinking can be quite difficult.

THE STRESSES OF FAMILY AND MONEY

Family trouble or personal financial problems cause stress that can seriously impair a manager's performance.

Deep financial difficulties may strike even among executives at the highest income levels. Dr. Rockett told us of a highly paid corporation president who plunged deeply into debt by living far beyond his means. He bought a luxurious yacht that he really couldn't afford. To get out of debt, he had to change his whole style of living.

Marital and family problems nearly always spill over into a manager's business affairs. For instance, two vice-presidents of a large oil company were both having trouble with their spouses, although neither was aware of the other's personal problems. These problems put both of them under such severe stress that they began quarreling over inconsequential business issues. Finally, their domestic situations were settled by a divorce in one case, and a revised marital relationship in the other. The trouble between the two executives quickly disappeared. Trouble with children and other relatives also can cause stress and have a significant effect on a manager's efficiency.

COMPANY ENVIRONMENT AS A CAUSE OF STRESS

Some companies maintain a supercharged emotional climate.

For some managers such companies can be exciting places to work. For others, they are hell on earth. These companies are frequently headed by ambitious, dedicated, and meticulous chief executive officers. People who work for such companies should pay close attention to how much stress they can tolerate.

Regardless of the causes of stress, managers can undertake a preventive program that will reduce the likelihood of a severe stress disorder.

The steps in this preventive program are discussed in the next chapter.

HOW TO DEAL
WITH EXCESSIVE STRESS

There are many different ways in which you can deal with
stress, including:

- Simple self-help countermeasures you can take on your
  own

- Help from a nonprofessional—such as a friend, colleague, spouse, or other relative

- Mutual approaches you can pursue with colleagues,
  friends, family, or a group of people who get together
  specifically to help one another

- Professional help from a physician, clergyman, or coun-
  selor

- Psychotherapy with a clinical psychologist or psychiatrist (A *psychiatrist* is a physician with psychological
  training; a *psychologist* has similar training, often with
  a doctoral degree in psychology, but is not a physician.)

- Drugs, including tranquilizers to relieve anxiety, and antidepressants to alleviate depression (These drugs are usually available only on prescription by a physician. Beware of all nonprescription medicines that purport to relieve tension or insomnia; they're usually ineffective and can be dangerous.)

Many, but not all, of these countermeasures are effective against both anxiety and depression. Of course, you should choose your countermeasures in relation to the severity of the stress and the problems it is causing. If one approach doesn't work for you, perhaps another will. There's no reason why you can't use several approaches simultaneously.

A psychologically oriented physician, a psychologist, or a psychiatrist can help you choose the best approach. In more severe cases, such professional advice should absolutely be sought. But there's no reason to wait until a stress problem arises before trying self-help measures. You should use them as preventive medicine. For example, every manager should get daily exercise and relaxation and should also develop outside interests.

MENTAL ATTITUDE

Distress often results from the thwarting of inner desires. Managers can prevent or relieve a great deal of distress by identifying their real psychological needs and acting on them. For example, Dr. Selye pointed out that egotism or selfishness is basic and natural to every human being. Because it's considered ugly, however, people try to deny its existence. This is often a major source of distress. Dr. Selye also explained that people have a deep, inborn craving for other people to recognize and approve what they do. Yet they are ashamed of this natural craving and try to deny it, which only leads to guilt feelings and distress.

Despite egotism and selfishness, most people are also motivated by an innate altruism. Dr. Selye has suggested that "altruistic egotism" as a philosophy of life can minimize distress. It means that managers can benefit themselves by helping other people and thus earning their respect.

Dr. Van Amberg points out that emotional conflicts over unselfishness and helping can pose serious problems. Many managers are by nature conscientious—and neglect their own needs, wants, and even their own welfare.

Managers who take an active role in the affairs of other people may be exploited or may simply intrude into the lives of others. Managers usually base their actions on the notion that selfishness is bad and unselfishness is good.

To resolve this problem, managers should know what their own welfare requires and take care of it. By taking good care of themselves, but at the same time being considerate of others, managers benefit all and promote harmony in their relationships with others in the office.

Sometimes a manager will say one of the following:

- "I can't take a vacation, because my colleagues and subordinates can't get along without me." (You should train your staff to handle matters in your absence.)

- "I can't let my trade association down. I will just have to serve another term as program chairman." (There are always other capable people who can serve.)

- "I have to do this or that for my spouse, my friends, or my children." (Usually they can do many things very well for themselves.)

The managers who do too much for others are drawing too heavily on personal energy reserves that they will need during times of crisis.

A more realistic view of what is selfishness and what is unselfishness can go a long way to help managers eliminate one of the root causes of stress. Dr. Van Amberg suggests these guidelines in giving help to others:

- *Give others help only if they ask for it.* Of course, this rule doesn't apply if someone obviously needs urgent assistance.

- *Help others only if you can do so without exhausting your time and energy.* Try to limit your help to a single occasion. Otherwise, the person being helped will probably ask for your assistance over and over again.

- *Avoid taking charge in a situation where only advice or assistance is required.*

- *Do not assume the receiver of help will be obligated to pay you back later on.*

COUNTERMEASURES A MANAGER CAN USE

The basic way for managers to reduce the pressure of time as a source of stress is to plan ahead and organize their work for maximum efficiency. This includes plugging leaks in their daily schedule, getting rid of useless routine and unnecessary paperwork, delegating to the maximum extent possible, and taking full advantage of available shortcuts. It particularly means avoiding last-minute crises by making decisions in advance whenever possible.

Reduction of working pressures is often essential to relieving anxiety, but work itself is often the best antidote to depression. When the source of depression is personal and not directly related to work, managers can help to ease their troubles by getting involved in chores they enjoy. Then, depression may quickly disappear.

If the basic cause of your distress is the fact that you are psychologically unsuited for your job and really want to do something quite different, however, you may have to make a major change in mid-career to be really happy. Sometimes high-ranking, highly successful people do this, even though it means giving up a considerable amount of income.

Manager's Daily Stress Identification Chart

The chart shown in Exhibit 13 will help you pinpoint the stressful events during your day. Some stresses are mild and some are strong, of course, but for the sake of simplicity, just add up the time you spend in any stressful situation. If the total is more than one and one-half hours per day for several days in a row, your health may be in jeopardy.

You can identify stresses that occur regularly and take steps to correct them. In the illustration given in Exhibit 13, the manager has had a very bad day indeed. But there is much in this schedule that can be corrected.

For example, the drive to work may be exhausting because of heavy traffic, but that can be remedied in several ways. The manager can join a car pool, hire a chauffeur, use public transportation, or even move closer to the office. The other events in this manager's schedule don't occur frequently. For example, the long lunch with the customer may take place only once a year. As long as it's an infrequent event, it should cause little trouble.

Like the manager in this illustration, you may be bothered by reading memos and studying reports. There are some steps you can take. You can have a subordinate brief you orally and give you a half-page summary in writing to back up the oral report. You could also have a trusted assistant study the memos and reports and give you a digest.

Exercise

Daily exercise is one of the most effective ways to prevent or relieve anxiety and depression. Exercise not only diverts you from activities or stimuli that cause disagreeable and excessive stress, but it also subjects you to a different, positive stressor and helps you get rid of aggression. Stress on one part of the body helps to relieve stress on another part. When you become frustrated and fatigued from struggling with a business problem, it's better to go for a swim than just sit down and rest. Also, emotional factors tend to turn stress into distress, while physical exercise has the opposite effect. Before undertaking any program of exercise, however, you should consult a physician for his or her advice.

The best exercise for overcoming stress and improving general health is vigorous activity that makes the lungs, heart, and blood vessels work hard. These are called aerobic exercises. They condition the body to consume oxygen more efficiently, improve blood circulation, strengthen the cardiovascular system, and thus help prevent heart attacks. Some aerobic exercises are running, swimming, bicycling, walking, running in place, handball, basketball, squash, tennis, golf, volleyball, lacrosse, soccer, rowing, wrestling, and fencing.

Manager's Daily Stress Identification Chart

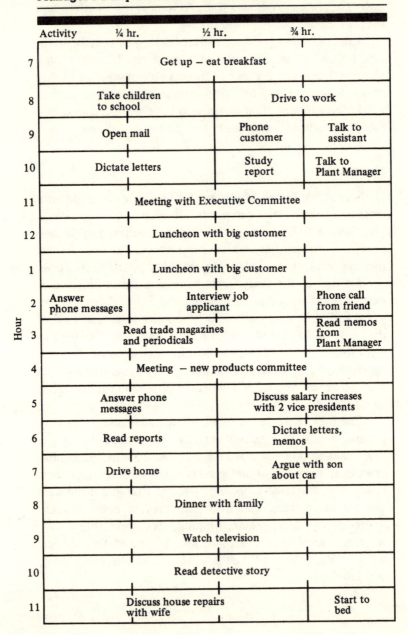

Hour	Activity	¼ hr.	½ hr.	¾ hr.
7	Get up — eat breakfast			
8	Take children to school		Drive to work	
9	Open mail		Phone customer	Talk to assistant
10	Dictate letters		Study report	Talk to Plant Manager
11	Meeting with Executive Committee			
12	Luncheon with big customer			
1	Luncheon with big customer			
2	Answer phone messages		Interview job applicant	Phone call from friend
3	Read trade magazines and periodicals			Read memos from Plant Manager
4	Meeting — new products committee			
5	Answer phone messages		Discuss salary increases with 2 vice presidents	
6	Read reports		Dictate letters, memos	
7	Drive home		Argue with son about car	
8	Dinner with family			
9	Watch television			
10	Read detective story			
11	Discuss house repairs with wife			Start to bed

Stress Response

| | ¼ hr. | ½ hr. | ¾ hr. |

Very
unpleasant
or rushed

Unpleasant
and tension
producing

Boring to
the point
that stress
occurs

Source: Adapted from
Robert J. Van Amberg,
*A Handbook of
Stress Disorders* ©
1962.

Diet

A regular, well-balanced diet is important to maintaining the high energy level needed to cope with stress. Dr. Van Amberg advises avoiding sugar as much as possible. While it gives a brief surge of energy, large amounts of sugar sometimes cause unfavorable complications, including marked weakness and trembling several hours after eating them. The best diet for adding to energy includes virtually no sugar and moderate starch, while emphasizing meat, fish, and vegetables. Certain protein concentrates prepared as a drink are helpful supplements. They, as well as peanuts, cheese, or a small piece of bittersweet chocolate help to stave off intense hunger between meals.

Sleep

Sufficient sleep is also essential to maintaining energy to deal with stress. Unfortunately, a principal symptom and effect of stress-induced anxiety is insomnia. If insomnia persists, consult a physician. Seven to nine hours' sleep is enough for most people. Fewer than seven hours may lead to fatigue for some individuals. More than nine hours in most instances not only is useless but may cause weakness. This can be a serious problem with stress-induced depression, in which excessive sleeping tends to be a principal symptom.

SIMPLE SELF-HELP MEASURES

You can use several measures on your own each day to relieve less severe anxiety or depression, or as an adjunct to other measures in more severe cases. These devices help put you in a frame of mind so you can say, "Today I am in control. I can manage this day on my own."

- *Temporarily block out problems.* You can develop the ability to put a stressful situation temporarily out of your mind. Concentrate on something strikingly different for a while before returning to the problem. Say, "It's okay for me not to be involved in that problem for the next hour because I can't handle it right now."

- *Follow an unconventional schedule.* You can change your working hours so that you work at the office very early in the morning or late at night, when you can concentrate on difficult tasks without the distractions that cause stress.

- *Write memos to yourself.* In a stressful situation, you should scribble out a forceful memorandum in brutally concise terms. Write down exactly what is disturbing you, naming specific persons and policies in the organization. You'll get feelings of aggression out of your system. Just writing the problem down often gives you a different perspective, makes the problem seem more manageable, and relieves stress. (By the way, don't send or read the memo to anyone else.)

- *Change your environment.* Consider taking twenty minutes off every day for aerobic exercise (with the approval of your physician) such as vigorous jogging, followed by a quick shower or swim. Or eat a leisurely lunch by yourself. Or, when stress builds up, try walking off the problem outside. The important thing is to change your immediate environment completely.

- *Concentrate on today's work.* When a job is so huge that the end of it can't be seen—but it must be done in three months—you must decide exactly how much to do today. Don't get sidetracked by what must be done months from now.

- *Find models and antimodels.* Pick out an executive in the company whom you consider a real success in dealing with complexities on the job. Think about why that person is successful and how he or she handles problems. Write these points down. Decide which techniques you can use in your own approach to stress. Then pick out another person who is definitely not a success. Think about (and write down) the reasons why that person fails to cope with problems. Then decide which of these reasons may apply to yourself.

- *Attack one problem at a time.* When several different problems or persons are simultaneously causing you stress, don't try to deal with more than one at a time. Instead, work out a strategy for coping with each of them independently. Otherwise, the result may be failure with all of them.

- *Develop new interests.* One of the best ways to control stress is to find another, completely different activity that you can turn to when you feel anxious or depressed. It might be a stamp or coin collection, a musical instrument, a handicraft, or a game. But it should be something that completely diverts your mind from whatever is causing stress. On a broader scale, you should develop interests that take you completely away from your job and give you a sense of fulfillment or accomplishment. These might be some form of community service; a scholarly, religious, or social organization; a theatrical or musical group; or perhaps a group sport.

Meditation

Spending a short time each day in one of several forms of meditation has been medically proven to be an effective way to reduce stress. One of the simplest forms, taught at the Menninger Foundation, includes three successive phases that you can practice alone or with others. This form of meditation can be used any time during the day, in your office or elsewhere, whenever stress builds up.

Relaxation Phase.   This first phase consists of five steps:

1. Sit quietly with your feet on the floor.

2. Close your eyes.

3. Progressive Relaxation: Tense every part of your body, one by one, starting with your toes and working progressively up to your head. Squeeze your eyes and mouth tightly closed. Then suddenly let go and relax all parts of your body simultaneously.

4. Sit quietly for a while.

5. Concentrate on various parts of your body that you normally ignore, such as the soles of your feet, your tongue, and your internal organs.

Meditation Phase.   With your eyes closed, simply concentrate on breathing, but don't force it. Eliminate thoughts of anything except breathing. Focus your attention on your nostrils and quietly "watch" the breath flowing in and out past your nostrils. Count each breath, first the inhalations from one to ten, and then the exhalations from one to ten. Continue this for ten to twenty minutes, at the end of which you can discontinue the meditation if you feel relaxed. You may open your eyes to check the time, but don't use an alarm. When you're finished, sit quietly for several minutes, first with your eyes closed and later with them open. Don't stand up for a few minutes. And don't worry about achieving a deep level of relaxation. Maintain a passive attitude and permit relaxation to occur at its own pace. When distracting thoughts occur, try not to dwell on them, and return to counting breaths. You can use this meditation once, twice, or several times a day, whenever you want to relax.

Guided Imagery Phase. To gain general psychological insights in addition to relaxation, go on to this phase instead of discontinuing the meditation after ten or twenty minutes. (Doing so at least once or twice a week, when you have the time, can be quite beneficial.) Think of yourself as a teenager and of the people who were then significant in your life. Hold imaginary conversations with them. Discuss your hopes and motivations. Repeat the same procedure for the later stages of your life.

Transcendental Meditation

Extensive medical research has proven that regular daily meditation helps people deal more effectively with stress. It relieves inner tension, lowers blood pressure, and generally improves physical as well as emotional health. Much research on this subject has been done by Herbert Benson, associate professor of medicine at Harvard Medical School and director of the Hypertension Section at Boston's Beth Israel Hospital.

Dr. Benson emphasizes that equally beneficial results can be obtained with several simple forms of meditation.

His early research was based on transcendental meditation (TM). His later research uses a breathing technique similar to the method taught by the Menninger Foundation, but instead of counting breaths, Dr. Benson's technique works like this: When breathing out, simply say the word "one" silently. For example, breathe in, then out, and say "one"; then breathe in and out again and repeat "one"; and so on. Breathe easily and naturally.

TM may be the most widely practiced form of meditation in the world. It derives from a two thousand-year-old Vedic tradition of India. It was brought to the United States and many other countries by Maharishi Mahesh Yogi.

TM is officially described as "a physiological state of deep rest, with closed eyes, in which the mind temporarily ceases the activity of the waking state, while cultivating a high degree of awareness and alertness."

Leaders of the TM movement contend that it must be taught by a qualified teacher in approximately six sessions. They do not publicly reveal exactly how it works. But based on information from several sources, we infer that the manager who wants to practice TM should do something like this:

- Sit in a comfortable position with your eyes closed. Ideally, you should become completely relaxed in about one minute.

- Focus your thoughts effortlessly on a simple, pleasant, meaningless one- or two-syllable sound. In the official course, the teacher selects this sound (called the mantra) for each student from the Sanskrit language, and it's not supposed to be revealed to anyone.

- If other thoughts intervene, let your mind drift back to the mantra, but do not concentrate on it. Your thoughts should be effortless.

- Eventually, your mind will *transcend* the mantra and veer to deeper sources of thought (like the ocean depths, with the surface currents representing conscious thinking).

- As you practice TM, you should become more skillful in minimizing mental activity so that your body settles into a state of rest deeper than deep sleep, while your mind remains clear and alert. According to TM theory, this allows the body to carry out repairs and adjustments not possible while normally awake or asleep.

- As you grow more proficient in TM, you should experience pleasant sensations and emotions. But some experts caution that excessive meditating can lead to hallucinations.

- Continue meditating for fifteen to twenty minutes. You may open your eyes to check the time, but don't use an alarm clock. When you're finished, sit quietly for several minutes, first with your eyes closed and later with them open.

- TM authorities recommend meditating twice a day, preferably before breakfast and dinner. But they say to discontinue it immediately if you experience adverse reactions such as headaches or upset stomach.

Self-hypnosis

A self-hypnosis process, called psychocybernetics, has been helpful to many people not only in relaxing, but also in achieving personal goals. You can practice it by devoting a short period each day to creating mental pictures of yourself that give you a realistic, positive self-image and thus help you achieve your goals of self-improvement and happiness. You form a picture in your imagination of the self you want to be and visualize yourself playing this new role. Your subconscious mind then helps you achieve this new image much better than you could by conscious effort. It helps you overcome negative self-images built up by unfavorable experiences in the past, often in childhood.

Psychocybernetics was developed by Maxwell Maltz, a New York plastic surgeon who discovered that his patients often acquired an entirely new personality along with a change in their physical appearance. The physical change also improves their self-image.

Dr. Maltz recommends practicing psychocybernetics for at least twenty-one days before evaluating its effectiveness. He says you should set aside at least thirty minutes a day to practice it. You should relax comfortably in an easy chair or lie down and put your imagination to work, picturing yourself as a completely worthwhile, successful, self-confident, relaxed, happy person, untroubled by worry, anxiety, depression, or feelings of inferiority. You should act out this role in detail in your imagination and let yourself respond emotionally. Try to relive your most successful experiences from the past, recalling them in vivid detail, including how you felt at the time.

Whenever you feel tension, anger, hostility, or depression during the day, you can take time out for a brief psychocybernetic "vacation," imagining yourself as calm, utterly relaxed, and at peace with the world.

A NOTE OF CAUTION

While meditation and self-hypnosis have been helpful in producing relaxation and relieving simple stress, at least three of the psychiatrists and psychologists we interviewed point out that these techniques do nothing to solve basic psychological problems that may underlie stress and depression. John F. O'Connor of Columbia, Daniel Levinson of Yale, and Harry Levinson of Harvard advise that self-help measures should not be used as a substitute for therapy by a qualified professional.

Dr. O'Connor cautions that you should not use either meditation or self-hypnosis without first consulting a physician. He notes that in rare instances these methods have caused serious side effects. For example, he said that in one experiment at the National Institute of Health, a patient using TM suddenly developed ventricular fibrillation—a heart condition that would have been fatal had not medical treatment been immediately available.

GETTING HELP FROM A FRIEND

You can probably deal with the normal stress of daily life entirely on your own. But why do so? It's nearly always easier to handle stress with some help.

Merely talking over routine stress problems with someone else may keep them from escalating. That someone may be a friend, colleague, spouse, or relative. That person serves as an outlet for expressing feelings that you would otherwise repress; for venting frustrations, aggressions, and anger that you would otherwise keep bottled up inside you. Repressing an emotion tends to magnify it and may worsen the physiological effects.

When you discuss your problems with another person, you should remember that your purpose is not to get advice on the psychological aspects of those problems. Unless the other person is specifically knowledgeable in psychology, the less advice he or she gives, the better.

That's why, as long as stress isn't causing difficult problems, the person in whom you confide need not have any psychological qualifications. He or she need only be a sympathetic, understanding, patient listener. Of course, a listener can be particularly helpful by asking questions and otherwise encouraging you to express your feelings.

The experts we interviewed agree that every manager should develop a close relationship with someone. But they also point out that doing so isn't easy. Dr. Daniel Levinson explained, "By their nature, business relationships discourage close personal friendships and frank expressions of feelings. If you are a manager, how can you be friends with others in your own company? You're competing for advancement with people at your own level, so you can't confide in them. You're trying to get the people above you to promote you, so you can't be frank with them about your problems. Nor can you be too candid with the people below you, over whom you must exercise authority." One possibility may be to confide in an older mentor from whom you seek no favor and over whom you exercise no authority, Dr. Levinson suggested. You might choose for instance, an older person no longer in the direct management chain, one who is assigned to special staff duties while nearing retirement. Or the mentor might be retired. "The answer may be to find an understanding, sympathetic friend in another occupation, business, or company," the Yale psychiatrist suggested.

INFORMAL GROUPS

Dr. O'Connor suggests another solution. You can meet periodically—perhaps weekly, or once or twice a month—for frank, confidential discussions with managers of other companies who are at approximately your own level. Sharing personal problems with such a group can be particularly helpful, since the other managers are likely to have problems similar to yours.

Dr. O'Connor emphasized, however, that the purpose of such a group is not to give psychological advice to one another. As experienced managers, the participants can undoubtedly give helpful advice on technical aspects of business problems that are causing stress. However, unless the group is headed by a qualified psychologist or psychiatrist, members should not probe too deeply into psychological aspects. To do so without professional guidance can have harmful effects. Some of Dr. O'Connor's patients have required intensive therapy to repair psychological damage done to them by ineptly led groups.

How can you find an informal group of compatible people who can help you deal with stress-related problems? Occasionally such groups are sponsored by a club, business association, church, or social organization. Dr. O'Connor pointed out a hazard in joining a group affiliated with a church. If psychological needs are subordinated to theological or religious issues, this could simply add to the stress you're already under.

HOW TO GET PROFESSIONAL HELP IN DEALING WITH EXCESSIVE STRESS

How do you know whether you need professional help in dealing with stress or stress-related problems? There's no sharp dividing line between the stress you can handle alone or by discussing problems with a sympathetic friend, and excessive stress that should be treated by a professional psychiatrist or psychologist. Particularly in a borderline case, the most significant symptoms occur within the individual manager, who is the only one who feels them. So, if that manager can recognize the symptoms, he or she is probably the best judge of whether or not therapy is in order. Symptoms like these would include:

- Severe physiological or psychological symptoms described in Chapter 10

- Prolonged periods of general anxiety, worrying, or brooding

- Unrelieved distress or brooding over a specific problem or defeat in business or personal life

- A general feeling of not performing as well as possible
- Specific, stress-related problems that are hindrances in business or personal life
- Feeling that problems in life are out of your control
- General difficulties in getting along with other people
- Serious difficulty in getting along with a certain person in particular
- An unexplained increase in family problems
- General feelings of unhappiness or dissatisfaction with life, or that life has passed you by
- A feeling of failure, or brooding over goals that you have not achieved and probably will never achieve
- Brooding over death
- Recurring thoughts of suicide

Everyone occasionally experiences such symptoms. Usually they don't last long or cause serious difficulty. But if even one of them persists or recurs with enough intensity, you should consider consulting a psychiatrist or psychologist. The main criteria are: do your problems significantly reduce or interfere with your performance on the job? Could you be more effective or have a better life if you got rid of the problems?

Your physician can probably refer you to a qualified expert for advice. A single diagnostic session with a psychiatrist or clinical psychologist should reveal whether you have problems that need to be treated. The expert who makes this diagnosis may continue to see you as a patient or may refer you to another therapist for treatment.

Others who can refer you to a psychiatrist or accredited psychologist for diagnosis or therapy include:

- Local medical societies
- Professional associations of psychiatrists or psychologists
- Psychiatric hospitals or clinics
- General hospitals with psychiatric departments
- Mental health associations
- Community mental health centers
- Medical schools
- Psychology departments of colleges and universities
- Psychological consulting organizations such as the Menninger Foundation, the Psychological Corporation, or Levinson Institute, which have affiliates in many countries.

CHOOSING A THERAPIST AND A THERAPY

The variety of psychological theories and individual or group therapy methods now available is so wide that selecting a therapist or a technique can be confusing and difficult. No single therapeutic method or theory is best for everyone, according to Joel Kovel, associate professor of psychiatry at Albert Einstein College of Medicine in New York. He points out, for example, that therapy based on Freud's psychoanalytic methods might be highly successful with one person, but may not work nearly as well with someone else who has a different personality.

Dr. Kovel contends, moreover, that the ability of the therapist is more important than the method of treatment. "Therapies all have their limits. But within these limits they are all designed to work if properly applied," he says. Also, harmful effects of treatment are more often due to an inept therapist than to the therapy itself, he declares. There are plenty of good therapists around, and also plenty of poor ones, Dr. Kovel says. Psychological therapists usually are not licensed. There's nothing to stop anybody from passing himself off as one. That's why a recommendation from a reputable source is important.

In selecting a therapist, keep in mind that the training a therapist has completed is significant, particularly if he or she received it at an institution that has high standards, according to Dr. Kovel. An advanced professional degree from a recognized school offers you some assurance as to this therapist's ability. All psychiatrists have a certain level of competence, because they have gone through so much training. After graduating from medical school, they completed long, comprehensive post-medical training. A therapist doesn't have to be a physician to be competent, however. Clincal psychologists and social workers, particularly those who have a doctorate degree in psychology, also receive intensive training.

Another important criterion is a therapist's accreditation by a professional association. For instance, Freudian psychoanalysts accredited by the American Psychoanalytic Association have to meet stringent requirements.

Before undergoing any treatment, you should ask for details concerning the therapist's training and accreditation, what therapeutic techniques he or she practices, and what psychological theories he or she espouses—such as the Freud, Jung, Adler, or Gestalt schools. These and other major schools of psychology are represented by their own professional associations, societies, or institutes in many countries. If you prefer to be treated according to a certain school, you can ask its professional group to recommend a therapist.

Many therapists don't specialize in any single school or method of therapy to the exclusion of all others. They use the approach that seems best for each patient, and they may combine elements of several schools and techniques.

No amount of training or accreditation can ensure that a therapist has the human characteristics needed to get the best results for you, Dr. Kovel says. Among the traits he cites: ability to sense what is going on inside another person; being attuned to communications in both directions; flexibility in adapting to changing circumstances without losing sight of basic purposes; ability to form rational judgments without shutting out feelings; and, most important, maturely caring for the patients' well-being.

PSYCHOLOGICAL SCHOOLS AND INDIVIDUAL THERAPY

Here is a brief summary of individual schools of psychology and methods of treating individual patients. It is based on Dr. Kovel's book, *A Complete Guide to Therapy*, and on interviews with him and other leading psychiatrists and psychologists.

Freudian psychoanalysis. Freud was the founder of modern psychological therapy. All other theories, schools, and methods of psychotherapy (such as those developed by Adler, Jung, Rank, Horney, Reich, Fromm, Perls, and Berne) either derive directly from Freudian psychoanalysis or get much of their impetus from Freud's ideas.

According to Freud's basic theories, human behavior is the combined result of conscious thought and unconscious drives and desires largely formed by experiences in early childhood. These unconscious factors have a heavy sexual connotation.

Freud developed the technique of psychoanalysis and used it exclusively in treating his patients. It's a deep, intensive process of curing psychological problems by dredging up the basic, unconscious drives behind them, recalling how those drives were formed, and understanding them. It consists of thoroughly analyzing the patient's personality and having the patient mentally relive the childhood experiences which influenced that personality.

The process requires a large investment of time and money. It involves three or four sessions a week for three or more years. During these sessions, patients endeavor to probe into their unconscious minds while lying on a couch, facing away from the analyst and saying whatever comes to mind. The analyst plays a passive role. By commenting on the patients' thoughts without leading them or rendering any judgment, the analyst helps the patient interpret those thoughts and overcome mental resistance to a free flow of thought.

Full-fledged psychoanalysis is used less frequently today than it was formerly. It's appropriate mainly for people whose lives are generally out of control or who have chronic diffused personality disorders—including sexual difficulties, deeply disturbed moods, and generally impaired personal relationships.

Such an intensive process is seldom necessary in treating managers' stress-related problems. In fact, Dr. O'Connor—who is a qualified psychoanalyst and favors a Freudian approach in his own practice—warns that delving too deeply into subconscious motivations is likely to be harmful to an ambitious, highly successful manager. Developing a thorough understanding of those motivations might result in overcoming them, with the result that the patient would no longer be effective as a manager.

To qualify as a Freudian psychoanalyst requires training that goes well beyond that of other psychiatrists and psychologists. Psychoanalysts must themselves have undergone thorough analysis.

Psychoanalytic psychotherapy. Freudian psychiatrists and psychologists today use therapeutic techniques that are less intensive than full-fledged psychoanalysis. They don't delve as deeply into the patient's subconscious or analyze all basic motivations. Instead, psychotherapy treats the problems and symptoms that result from those underlying drives.

During the sessions, which may be held only once or twice a week, the patient usually sits in a chair and faces the therapist. They hold a two-way discussion of the patient's symptoms, problems, and reactions, with the therapist playing a more active role than in psychoanalysis.

Psychotherapy may continue as long as the patient's problems interfere with his or her effectiveness or happiness. The patient may need psychological support for a few months or for several years.

People who have chronic difficulty in coping with the stresses of daily living may need psychotherapy indefinitely. They may see a therapist each week for many years to get help in keeping problems under control. Or, if their emotions follow a pattern of peaks and valleys, they may discontinue therapy whenever the problems subside and then resume it whenever they recur.

Psychoanalytic psychotherapy can help an individual who has deep-rooted, specific psychological problems that cause serious difficulties and that may become aggravated under heavy stress.

Dr. O'Connor advises that, unless a manager has such problems, even psychotherapy can be harmful, if too extensive. The subconscious drives and aggressions that cause difficulty may also impel a person to fight for success. Too much insight into these inner feelings may reduce an individual's effectiveness as a manager.

Brief, goal-oriented psychotherapy. Dr. O'Connor believes this approach is the best one for you as a manager. Although based on psychoanalytic techniques, it does not delve deeply into psychological problems. Instead, the therapist merely helps you alleviate those problems that interfere with your performance. For example, Dr. O'Connor noted, if you are suffering from fear of failure in an important assignment, you may take it out on your subordinates by becoming irritable with them. Or you may clash with a superior or someone of equal rank. Or you may become depressed. To overcome such a problem without trying to root out any deep, subconscious factor behind it might take only three or four therapy sessions, Dr. O'Connor explained.

Neo-Freudian analysis. Psychologists and psychiatrists who follow the Adler, Sullivan, and Horney schools differ from Freudians mainly by de-emphasizing subconscious thought and sexual repression. Their therapeutic techniques focus on specific goals, unrealistic attitudes, social relationships, self-assertion, self-regard, and coping with everyday psychological needs. Their methods would be beneficial to a manager who prefers a more pragmatic approach to his or her problems.

The Jungian school. Based on the ideas of the late Swiss psychiatrist C. G. Jung, this school acknowledges an even deeper subconscious than Freud's—a sort of collective unconscious rooted in the history of the human species. This approach uses analysis of dreams as the key to bringing patients into contact with their subconscious minds. The couch is not used, and sessions usually continue once or twice a week for a year or more. Besides deep exploration of dreams, the Jungian method includes down-to-earth, less far-reaching, supportive psychotherapy. The therapist plays a very active role and gets personally involved.

Jungian therapy may be particularly beneficial to you if you seek an enlightened perspective on your life in addition to relief from psychological distress. But its success hinges on your willingness to believe in its basic premises, which verge on the mystical.

Gestalt and Rogerian therapies, the existential approach and human potential movement.   While they vary somewhat from each other, all these approaches are quite pragmatic. They reject or pass over concepts of subconscious drives or suppressed desires. They emphasize direct experience, self-awareness, and active acceptance of the current situation.

The existential approach, which is popular in Central Europe, contends that anxiety is caused simply by not facing reality, and the only cure is to face it, no matter how horrible it is. The starting point of all psychotherapy must be the present, the here and now.

Gestalt therapy, which is very popular in California, is existential but not gloomy like European existentialism. It stresses active awareness of the present as a means of healing. It encourages patients to express openly all their needs and resentments as the way to get rid of guilt feelings and make life easier. It frequently employs dramatization or role-playing.

Suppose, for instance, that you are the patient undergoing Gestalt therapy. You might shift back and forth between two chairs. You play your conscience in one chair, yelling at your imaginary self in the other chair, ordering it to do better. You then move to the other chair and play an obstinate underdog, spitefully defying your conscience. Gestalt therapy emphasizes highly emotional interaction between people. It can induce a state of near hysteria.

The human potential movement, which started in California, combines existentialist emphasis on direct experience with the ideal of the perfectibility of humanity. It advocates spontaneity, self-expression, and emotional honesty. Its ultimate goal is personal happiness.

Rogerian therapy—founded by Carl Rogers, a former Christian evangelist—is a humanist approach that features intense belief in the goodness of people. The therapist must experience what the patient is experiencing and adopt, in Rogers's words, "unconditional positive regard" for the patient. The fundamental purpose of Rogerian therapy is to get people to feel better about themselves by counteracting their bad self-images with the therapist's positive regard for them. Rogers sees therapy as equivalent to good education. The Rogerian therapeutic process is brief—usually one session a week for a year or less.

Gestalt and existentialist approaches are reported to work best with managers who feel that their emotions are pent up, whose lives are deficient in emotional intensity, whose personal relations have become stultified, or who feel estranged from the world.

The human potential movement and Rogerian therapy are said to work best for managers bothered by feelings of loneliness, inferiority, or insecurity, but whose problems aren't severe, and for those whose treatment need not go very deep.

Biofeedback.   This method of training in relaxation is based on the theory that a person can consciously control certain body functions that have been thought to be controlled by the involuntary nervous system. Sophisticated scientific equipment measures the patient's relaxation by monitoring blood pressure, pulse rate, muscle tension, and skin temperature as well as the brain's alpha waves. The equipment feeds back information on these body changes while the therapist teaches the patient how to relax the muscles of the body and the thought processes. The results are similar to those experienced during deep meditation.

This process, which is taught in about ten sessions, is said to train managers to control their own stress levels. At each session, the therapist has the individual think about particularly stressful situations—dealing with a difficult customer, perhaps, or preparing a report for the company chairman. As the manager thinks about each situation, the therapist explains how to control physical and mental reactions. At the same time, the equipment monitors the effect of this procedure on the vital functions. By the end of the training, the manager may be able to control his or her reactions without being told how.

Herbert Benson's experiments at Boston's Beth Israel Hospital confirm that the biofeedback technique can lower blood pressure, but he points out that other techniques, such as meditation, can accomplish the same results without the use of scientific equipment.

Behavioral therapy.   A number of therapies treat observable symptoms—such as stuttering in a stressful situation, or a fear or phobia—rather than the underlying psychological problems that cause those symptoms. The American Psychological Association considers the behavioral approach one of the most important forces in therapy today.

One of the best known behavioral techniques is *behavior modification*, which has many applications. It is used in mental hospitals to treat psychotic patients; in business firms to change employees' behavior—for instance, to increase their productivity or to discourage chronic tardiness. It's based mainly on giving rewards for desirable behavior (positive reinforcement) and punishing or withdrawing rewards for undersirable behavior (negative reinforcement). The rewards range from simple praise to special privileges to increased pay.

A therapist might use behavior modification to overcome a stressful relationship between two managers by showing how they can reinforce each other's behavior in ways that eliminate conflict between them. Or the therapist could help managers reinforce their own behavior so as to reduce stress. For example, suppose that you habitually waste time because you neglect to plan each day's activities properly. You could give yourself some enjoyable reward on days when you do plan efficiently, but withhold that reward on days when you fail to plan your schedule. The reward might be to eat lunch at your favorite restaurant or to watch a TV show you especially enjoy.

Another behavioral therapy, called *systematic desensitization*, is effective in treating fears and phobias. If you fear a certain task because it's unusually stressful, a therapist might help you build up to it in easy steps. You would start by performing a simplified version of the task that's beneath your ability. Then a slightly more difficult version, and so on, until you can perform the full task with ease.

Behavioral therapy may be the best way for a manager to deal with stress-related problems if psychotherapy does not appeal to him or her. It also may be the answer when the urgency of the situation dictates faster results than can be obtained by conventional psychotherapy.

Drug therapy. Drug therapy—including the use of tranquilizers and sedatives for anxiety and tension, tricyclic antidepressants for deep depressions, and other psychologically active drugs—is considered a form of behavioral therapy. Drugs temporarily relieve symptoms of more serious stress-related problems. They don't solve the underlying problems, however, and they involve several risks. They can dull emotional pain so that basic problems become much more difficult to treat. Also, the patient may become addicted to a tranquilizer or sedative, which adds a new problem to the old one.

Primal therapy. This method was developed in Southern California by Arthur Janov, who formerly practiced Freudian and neo-Freudian therapy. He says the inception of his theory came during a session with a patient. On a hunch, Janov urged the patient to call out "Mother" or "Daddy." The patient did so and then began an infantile crying bout that culminated in a "piercing, deathlike scream that rattled the walls of my office," Dr. Janov recalls. Afterward, the patient felt much better.

Dr. Janov contends that all psychological troubles are the result of hurts and wrongs done to young children by their parents. He says these troubles can be cured by getting patients to expel their deep-rooted, poisonous feelings toward their parents through wrenching, painful, infantile screams.

The intensive phase of the treatment lasts three weeks, during which patients live in a hotel, totally removed from their regular activities. They abstain from all drugs or diversions that might reduce tension. Each patient has a two- to three-hour session with the therapist each day. Each session ends when the therapist decides the patient has reached an emotional peak. Any form of therapy other than screaming is forbidden during the session. There is no discussion of problems or behavior, no exploration of fantasies or analysis of feelings. After this phase, patients return to their normal lives but continue treatment for about six months with a primal group. The participants hold no conversations with one another. In fact, they have as little to do with each other as possible. All of the people in the room simply spend the period screaming at their parents.

GROUP THERAPY

All the psychological theories and therapeutic approaches described so far in this section can be used either with individuals or with groups of patients. Full-fledged Freudian psychoanalysis is so deep and intense that it's nearly always done individually. In biofeedback and primal groups, there's very little direct contact or interaction between group members. But group therapy plays a prominent role in the neo-Freudian schools, Gestalt therapy, and the human potential movement. In addition, several other approaches are distinctly group aproaches.

Group therapy has an important advantage over individual therapy and a significant disadvantage. The advantage: group therapy introduces a social dimension to psychotherapy. Stress-related problems are often rooted in a person's relationships with other people. So group members' interactions with one another often bring special insights into their feelings and provide corrective emotional experiences that aren't possible in individual therapy. The disadvantages: group therapy can never probe as deeply into a patient's inner feelings as individual therapy can.

In traditional group psychotherapy, the therapist leads and guides the sessions, but the group members play the most important role in one another's therapy. The group typically has ten to twelve members. They sit on comfortable chairs and couches around the room, perhaps the therapist's office, facing one another. The session may last two to three hours, although some groups occasionally hold additional marathon sessions that continue as long as twenty-four to forty-eight hours, with only brief periods of relaxation. The emphasis is on group members' uninhibited expression of their problems, feelings, and reactions to one another. They comment frankly and try to get at the psychological reasons for their reactions. Sometimes their blunt comments evoke strong emotional responses from other members. Generally, the more emotional the meeting becomes, the more successful it is in getting to the roots of the members' problems.

The therapist asks probing questions and makes provocative statements intended to elicit reactions from group members, particularly members who remain passive or withdraw from the discussion. The therapist also prevents any one member from dominating the meeting, but otherwise interferes as little as possible.

Of course, groups differ in their methods and procedures, based on each therapist's approach and therapeutic technique. Backgrounds, personalities, ages of the members, and the nature of their problems also make a difference.

Sometimes a therapist provides individual treatment for members of a group. This would seem to combine the advantages of both approaches. But it doesn't always work that way. The effects of one can counteract the effects of the other.

Unfortunately, the quality of group therapy varies as widely as other types of treatment. There's nothing to stop anyone from starting a group. Many groups have been started by people who lack psychological training. An inexpertly led group can result in devastating psychological damage to participants. You should check thoroughly on the therapist's credentials before undergoing any group therapy.

Some Group Approaches to Psychotherapy

Following is a summary of some group approaches:

T-Groups. The "T" stands for "training." This is a psychotherapeutic program designed especially for business executives and managers. It provides a laboratory in which participants can help one another deal with problems of discipline, decision-making, leadership, and interpersonal relations.

Albert J. Marrow, a leading New York psychologist, tells us that T-Groups follow the behavioral school of psychology. He said that psychologists who conduct them must have special training in group psychotherapy and group leadership.

In a typical T-Group, fifty or sixty individuals meet for five days and nights of intensive lectures. The large group is then divided into small groups of about ten persons each for therapy sessions. The best T-Groups are composed of managers, each of whom comes from a different company, so they can be open and frank with one another. The technique has also been used with managers who all come from the same company. Each T-Group is led by a well-qualified psychologist whose main function is to help the participants express and understand their feelings and not repress them. The purpose is to reveal to members as much as possible about their own behavior through self-diagnosis and comparing perceptions of each other's behavior.

People attend T-Groups primarily to develop more awareness of themselves and change the way they relate to others. In the sessions they develop increased sensitivity to the feelings of others and learn to humanize their relations in business.

T-Groups have no fixed agenda and no fixed rules. They decide their own procedures. However, most of them lean heavily toward role-playing.

People who benefit most from T-Groups tend to have:

- Relatively strong egos that are not overwhelmed by internal conflicts

- Defenses sufficiently low to allow them to hear what others say about them

- The ability to communicate thoughts and feelings

Encounter Groups. These groups are established to help healthy, stable people get more joy, warmth, meaning, and spontaneity into their lives. People usually don't join encounter groups as patients seeking help with emotional problems.

Transactional Analysis. This method was developed by the late Eric Berne, a psychiatrist who practiced in San Francisco. Transactional analysis (TA) is based on the idea that in every person there are three "ego states" derived from earlier experience. These are called the *Parent*, the *Adult*, and the *Child*. Each represents different values and ways of dealing with the world. When a "transaction" occurs between two people—that is, one person says or does something that provides a stimulus for the other person to respond—any one of the three possible ego states may be operating in either of the two persons. TA analyzes such transactions to determine which ego states lead to specific stimuli and responses. Once this is known, unsuccessful transactions can be explained and often avoided in the future.

The *Parent* ego state is often described as the teaching, lecturing, "being-right" side of a person. It consists of behaviors and attitudes one has learned from parents or other authority figures.

The *Adult* is objective and rational. It is in the adult state that one learns from experience, thinks, and bases attitudes and behaviors on these experiences.

The *Child* is highly emotional and uses both passive and aggressive means to obtain gratification.

An ideal transaction involves the rational, thinking, Adult ego states of the two persons involved. Other less than ideal transaction patterns may also be acceptable. As long as both persons are operating in the same ego state, there is no conflict. In a complementary transaction, a manager acting in the Adult ego state might speak to an employee who is in the Child ego state. As long as the employee does not resent this treatment, and responds in the same mode, there is two-way communication without conflict. Trouble arises, however, when the lines of communication get crossed— for example, if a manager addresses an employee as Adult to Adult but gets a response from Child to Parent. According to one analyst, most conflict situations involve the Parent or Child ego state. The objective of transactional analysis is to give people insight into these situations so that they can convert all transactions into the ideal Adult-Adult mode.

The goal of TA is to foster a mature, realistic Adult ego state, rather than the ego of a harsh, enjoining Parent or an impulsive, selfish Child.

Therapy sessions, usually held weekly over a ten-week period, feature a no-nonsense approach. The leader plays a down-to-earth role. There's a lot of give and take by everybody, and good humor is the rule. There is no attempt at deep probing into one's personality to develop self-awareness. The leader stays close to the level of the members of the group. The approach is educational and pragmatic. It features positive thinking carried beyond the "unconditional positive regard" of Rogerian therapy.

Psychodrama. This complex procedure, developed by J. L. Moreno, is based on the assumption that all human beings need to play certain psychological roles in their relationships with others. For instance, an emotionally troubled youth may need to play the role of a perfect, highly achieving hero to his mother, but may need to become an abject, passive failure to his father. Moreno's method lets people re-create these conflicting roles in a controlled group therapy setting. Participants play roles that attack a problem from several different angles until it is mastered.

The therapist is called the director. He or she changes scenarios in accordance with whatever patients reveal at any particular time. The technique resembles Gestalt therapy. However, instead of focusing on awareness, it emphasizes the re-creation of problems in living.

After a dramatic session, the participants usually get together for a regular group meeting in which they discuss their feelings and relate the dramatic situations to their everyday life.

Family therapy. This is a form of group therapy in which the group is an actual family. The technique is becoming increasingly popular for two reasons: the family can be an ideal unit for ferreting out psychological problems and treating them; the need for such treatment is widespread, as can be seen in the breakdown of family life in today's industrialized societies. The method promotes more mature relationships within the family and more responsible attitudes toward other people.

A FINAL NOTE

Some psychiatrists and psychologists who follow traditional schools and use conventional methods of psychotherapy question the value of more recently developed, less conventional methods.

These newer methods should not be used for really serious psychological problems. For instance, behavior modification, T-Groups, encounter groups, and transactional analysis make no pretense of probing deeply into the human mind.

A number of these less conventional methods, however, have helped people cope with stress and lead happier lives, when there is no deep problem. If you merely seek general help in handling stress, you might want to consider the newer methods, provided the therapist is a fully qualified psychologist or psychiatrist. Be wary of any approach or technique that is ballyhooed as a panacea or as the best or only answer to psychological problems.

PART III

CONTROLLING TIME

INTRODUCTION

Do you remember the last time you were deeply absorbed in a project and were startled to realize that what you had thought was fifteen minutes of concentration had really been an hour? And do you remember the last time you were at a meeting when the talk wandered on about things that really didn't interest you, and you kept looking at your watch because you were sure it had stopped?

We have all had such personal experiences that seem to belie the objective nature of time. The truth is that our subjective perception of time is the real key to effective time management. For we all have roughly the same number of hours and minutes in our workdays. It is what we do in, and with, each minute of those hours that determines whether we will accomplish our goals or fail to meet them; whether we will flow easily from one task to the next or always be out of step with the present; whether we will feel relaxed or driven most of the time.

In Part III, you'll be asked to take a long, hard look at the way in which you utilize your time. The results may be shocking or even disturbing, but by the time you've finished, you'll be on your way to a better understanding of your use of time and what effective utilization of working hours can do for you and your career.

14

WAYS OF
LOOKING AT TIME

Time is at once both elastic and rigid. Different people, at different times, have developed all sorts of approaches to this seeming paradox. Even the clichés about time indicate its complex nature: time flies, on borrowed time, working against time, time crawls, in the nick of time, and—at times—time stands still.

Even in the practical matter of using time, we are contradictory: we say we have no time when we have much to do, yet we believe the old saying, "If you want something done, give it to a busy person." How any one person perceives time is a function of moment-to-moment changes in moods, circumstances, pressures, responsibilities, obligations, and dreams.

Given such subjectivity, such diversity of perception and reaction, it would seem almost impossible to come to any common basis for understanding and using time. And yet we do—all the time. Across cultural lines, the amount of time a person can expect to live is roughly the same, whether measured in moons, suns, or years, seasons or rainfalls. Even cultures with different calendars all have twenty-four hour days, roughly divided into sleeping and waking hours. Furthermore, each culture imposes on its members specific ideas about how they are to spend those waking hours.

The different images of the nature of time reflect the ways in which people spend their waking hours. Following are six of the most common of these images:

1. Time as your master

2. Time as your enemy

3. Time as a mystery

4. Time as your slave

5. Time as your referee

6. Time as a neutral force

Chances are, at some period or moment of your life, you have subscribed to each. The following discussion will help you analyze the implications of each attitude in terms of your own personal effectiveness.

TIME AS YOUR MASTER

When you see time as your master, you are abdicating responsibility for your life to this great, external force. "The dictates of time" is not an idle phrase, but rather a statement of belief in the power time has over one. So are these similarly fatalistic statements: "It's just a matter of time," "Only time will tell," and "Time waits for no one." This attitude puts time in the driver's seat, with you as willing or unwilling passenger.

If you regard yourself as a slave to time, you may recognize the following types of behavior:

- Giving up on something because it is "too late" or "too early" for you to do it, even though you would really like to. You might, for example, forgo a party or a card game because you know it will keep you up past your usual bedtime even though you would enjoy going. Or it could mean refusing a pleasurable late afternoon tennis date because it would mean leaving the office before your habitual quitting time.

- Conforming to rigid, clock-linked personal habits, no matter what. For example, some people get up at exactly the same time each morning, regardless of what they have to do that day or how much they might prefer to get more rest. Others habitually eat lunch precisely at noon every day even if they are not really hungry at that hour.

- Sticking to a predetermined schedule, even when you could easily skip part of it in favor of something you would rather do. One manager attending a convention, for instance, left a session he was deeply involved in because it ran over the allotted time period, even though the next session he had planned to attend was much less central to his interests. Another manager insists on making the 5:45 P.M. commuter train each day, even if it means rushing, rather than relax and catch the 5:55 or the 6:05.

- Relying on the clock rather than on other cues to determine what it is appropriate for you to do. Some professionals believe that an hour is the right amount of time for a meeting, no matter what the subject matter or level of intensity of the discussion. Others feel uneasy when long-distance calls extend longer than, say, ten minutes, even when the call is saving days of traveling or meeting time.

The benefit of this kind of behavior is that it limits your choices. Superficially at least, life is easier when you have fewer choices to make. In these cases, you might sit back passively and say, "It's not up to me—the clock says so."

But there are many drawbacks to this attitude toward time. By abdicating your responsibility for minute-to-minute choices, you erect rigid bars around yourself. These bars do serve as some protection from possible confusion, uncertainty, and risk. But they can block out opportunities for spontaneity, growth, and even professional breakthroughs. For, when you allow time to be your master, you consign all other values and goals to second place.

TIME AS YOUR ENEMY

If you see time as your enemy, you are spoiling for a fight. We talk with finality of "beating the clock," as though by gaining a few minutes or hours we could accumulate them as capital. Yet time relentlessly marches on.

Here are some kinds of behavior that are typical of people who are trying to beat time:

- Playing personal games with deadlines, games that are external to the actual demands of the task. For example, there is the manager who enjoys the morning drive to work, but keeps trying to find shortcuts to "set a record." Or the individual who labors mightily to meet short, self-imposed deadlines for work assignments, even when no one else cares about getting that particular work done early.

- Feeling triumphant about being early, and beaten by being late. The gratification or mortification here has to do only with the timing itself, not the purpose for which the time was intended. For example, some managers make a habit of appearing early for meetings, even though it means they must wait for everyone else to arrive. Others feel chagrin when they are even a few minutes late for an appointment—not because of the inconvenience to the other person, but because of what they see as their own loss in their battle against time.

- Resenting others who take a different attitude toward time. People who see the process of using time as a battle become annoyed when other people approach time more casually. For example, statements such as "There's no rush" or "We have plenty of time" are immediate irritations to them, even if they are absolutely true.

- Judging others on their efficient use of time rather than on their effectiveness. When the defeat of time becomes a paramount value, a manager is likely, for example, to value more a subordinate who gets quick results than one who probes deeper to determine the right things to do. The same manager might prefer a colleague who runs precisely timed meetings over another whose group sessions are more flexible, regardless of the content or outcome of either.

One advantage of viewing time as an enemy is that it stirs up the spirit of competitiveness that many believe is the key to achievement.

The biggest drawback to battling time, of course, is the inevitability of eventual failure. But there are also immediate negative consequences. When your mind is in a nearly constant state of war, you cannot fully apreciate your experiences, your relationships, even your achievements and delights. It will become difficult for you to live in the present if your mind is ever on your strategy for the next skirmish. Satisfactions become fleeting, life grim.

TIME AS A MYSTERY

When you view time as a mystery, you allow it to become something outside of your conscious concerns. And so the only way to deal with time is to try to work around it, hoping it won't get in your way. This approach to time is similar to a common attitude to the body. For instance, you may not be consciously aware of your stomach until something goes wrong with it, until it starts to hurt. Viewing time as a mystery sometimes works to our advantage. But every so often the power of time seems to descend from somewhere external to wreak havoc with our plans and ambitions.

Here are some types of behavior that usually accompany the notion that time is a mystery:

- Concentrating intensely on the task at hand. The laboratory scientist is an obvious example of this singleness of purpose. And so is every manager at times when one task supersedes all other considerations.

- Regarding with suspicion and perhaps envy people who take other attitudes toward time. If time seems beyond your control, it may be difficult for you to deal with other people whose relationship to time is more direct.

- Worrying about unforeseen consequences. When time seems a mystery, it becomes difficult to predict what its passage will imply. When time seems to come and go without rational explanation, one cannot accurately project needs, resources, or the reactions of others. This attitude is prevalent in even the most rational people in situations of sudden, intense, or widespread change when many previously fixed reference points shift quickly.

- Refusing to make firm time commitments. If you are faced with trying to do something you have never done before, time may suddenly become a mystery. You don't know how long each phase will take or when you will finish the task. For some people, this attitude is habitual. They see many tasks and activities as being "new" and unpredictable.

The attraction of approaching time as a mystery lies in the belief that by ignoring time you can prevent it from becoming a problem, thus allowing you to concentrate on the tasks and problems at hand. By not worrying about time, you convince yourself that you can concern yourself exclusively with what is to be done.

The drawback to this approach is that time does exist for each person in finite amounts. Unless one recognizes the scarcity of time, one may find oneself spending time on various tasks and activities out of proportion to one's preferred priorities.

TIME AS YOUR SLAVE

When you view time as your slave, your central concern becomes control. You attempt to determine how long you will permit use of your time for each possible choice. But since time is an elusive force, this approach requires set structures and constant discipline. This attitude can be recognized by the following types of behavior:

- Living in the future. When each day or each week seems to require taming by your will, you necessarily must concern yourself with planning your time. Since each day is charted, present time requires only that you carry out your plans, while focusing your real energies on perfecting the plan for a future day or week. Meetings provide excellent examples of this phenomenon in action. Instead of immersing themselves in the discussion, people often think about what they will say next, what they will do when the meeting is over, what plans they can make to implement what is presently being talked about.

- Feeling guilty or ashamed of spontaneity. If you need to exercise total control over time, you may feel that you have failed if you give into the temptation of a detour from your plans, a break in discipline. Many a manager, for example, sitting longer than planned at an eminently productive business lunch, feels slothful rather than satisfied.

- Placing great value on activity and visible results. If you are determined to master time, you will need constant, visible proof of your control over it. And so the more flurries of activity, the more dramatic their outcomes, the more external evidence there is that you are indeed extracting all you can from your time. Do you ever express your satisfaction in statements like these? "I didn't let up for one minute all day today" or "No one else believed I could have the report finished by Friday."

- Feeling weighted down by responsibilities. Ownership, possession, control, and mastery can all be burdens to bear. If you feel the need to squeeze the maximum results from every second of your time, you will frequently experience exhaustion. Results you want to achieve carry the added weight of proof of your own self-determination. The individual who takes work along on vacations is showing this attitude. And so is the manager who cannot delegate work to subordinates; he or she fears the loss of control.

The attractions of this attitude toward time are among the most widely sanctioned by Western society. This attitude is supposed to be the underpinning of industriousness and achievement. It provides a standard and measure of individual worth. And it provides a simple set of personal values: it is good to use time efficiently; it is bad to waste it in ways that are not visibly productive.

The drawbacks to the belief that time can be enslaved are beginning to become evident in various ways throughout Western society. People are questioning the purpose of much activity that has been automatically approved. More and more people are complaining of the constraints they feel are placed on their own humanity by an ethic that recognizes only visible achievements.

TIME AS YOUR REFEREE

When you see time as a referee, you are setting it up as the judge of your life. You are investing time not only with power but also with a range of emotions to which you must respond appropriately. The hands on the clock signal times for pleasure, displeasure, eager expectation, or utter despair—and those who take this attitude toward time will respond in kind. Here are some of the ways this is done:

- Requiring access to absolute chronological accuracy. Some people invest in precision watches; others furnish their homes and offices with a variety of clocks to be ceremoniously wound and set; still others frequently turn on the radio to learn the hour. These actions all ensure that the person is in synchronization with the referee, getting precisely the right signals.

• Cheating and covering up. Even if you give time the authority of a referee, you will not like its "decisions." So people use phrases such as "sneaking a break" or "stealing a moment" to indicate that they feel they ought not to be doing what they are doing; they want to and will do it anyway; and they expect, but somehow hope to escape, the punishment they feel they deserve.

• Desiring to please the external authority. Psychologically, the clock comes to represent the parent, teacher, or boss. People in such a frame of mind do not look at their watches for neutral information; rather, they see what time it is and smile, or frown, or become agitated at the implicit message in the instrument.

• Indulging in periodic changes in activity. People who see time as a referee sometimes feel the need to stop playing the game for a while. This can explain the incongruous behavior of the fastidious and meticulous worker who spends holidays climbing mountains and growing a beard. Or the very conscientious employee who, without having shown any symptoms of illness, calls in sick right after completing a taxing assignment.

The attraction of this attitude toward time is that it provides a set rhythm by which to pace one's life. Just as a metronome assists in piano practice, the clock provides a continuing reference point for various other exertions.

The big drawback, however, is that the human mechanism is too complex to be judged accurately simply on its timing. Internal rhythms are various and changing. People who try hard to mold their behavior to the clock eventually find that they do not reach their own potentials, to the detriment of themselves and also of their work.

TIME AS A NEUTRAL FORCE

Time is a resource we are all blessed with at birth. It is like air, in the sense that it is there to sustain us; like fingers and hands, in the sense that the possible uses of it are as varied and complex as our imaginations and wills allow.

Minutes and hours, even weeks and years are convenient divisions of time that give people some common basis for sharing and understanding what happens to time, and for arranging what they hope to have happen.

The flow of our own personal time is important to each of us. The ticking of the clock is useful, but not of primary human value. And so if you can overcome a concern with specific hours and minutes, you will be better able to recognize your time as a whole. Then you can take full responsibility for your time—and do what you really want with it.

What follows is a step-by-step guide to help you stop seeing time as a master, or as an enemy, or as a mystery, or as a slave, or as a referee. Rather, if you put yourself into the pages to come, you will recognize time as a personal yet neutral resource that simply exists until you determine what you want to make of it.

15

HOW TO DETERMINE THE WAY YOU ARE SPENDING YOUR TIME

Each week has 168 hours. Each individual creates a unique schedule from that resource. Before you can determine how to enhance the usage of your time, you must know how you are using it now.

You may believe you know how you are currently apportioning your time. But in a recent Alexander Hamilton Institute survey of top managers, 25 percent of those who had ever kept a time log reported that they were surprised by the results they obtained. Perhaps even more convincing of the value of a study of time usage, 87.5 percent of the survey respondents said that their time logs proved helpful in understanding the time problems they had.

This section will give you two separate tools for analyzing how you are presently spending your time. The data you generate from these investigations will provide your own starting point for this book's subsequent guidance in enhancing your use of time. Even if you fail to make use of these tools, that guidance will still be helpful. If you devote yourself to the self-investigation, however, this book will have more immediate and practical value.

THE FIVE BASIC LIFE ACTIVITIES

1. Work

2. Sleep

3. Family and social life

4. Hobbies, recreation, and interests

5. Community, religious, or charitable work

It is useful to see these areas as separate and distinct from one another. Exhibit 14, "Current Division of My Time," will help you visualize these areas graphically.

Please fill out Exhibit 14 for the next week as follows:

- *Start tomorrow.* There is no need to wait for the beginning of the week; just start with the appropriate day and fill in the spaces for seven days.

- *Make a copy of the chart.* This is preferable to using the form in this book, for you may wish to do this exercise again at a later date.

- *Collect five writing instruments of different colors.* You can use pens, pencils, crayons, markers, or any combination thereof. Just be sure that the marks of the five instruments you select look noticeably different from one another on paper.

- *Put the copy of Exhibit 14 and the five writing tools next to your bed* or anywhere else they will be conveniently accessible at the very end of your day.

- *Fill out the color key at the bottom of Chart 1.* Use one of your writing instruments for each of the five basic life activities. Make a mark of a different color in each of the boxes.

- *At the end of each day, fill in each hour for that day.* Fill in each hour's square in the color representing the activity you spent that hour on. Some activities may fall into one of several categories. For example, a meal eaten alone may be "recreation," while a family dinner would be "family life," and a business lunch would be "work." It is, of course, possible to divide a box into two, three, or four parts, if you spent just a fraction of an hour on each activity. But do not be concerned about accounting for every five minutes; the purpose of the chart is to give you an overall picture.

- *Fill out the chart each night for seven consecutive days.* At the end of the week, you will have a meaningful mosaic showing the true division of your time that week. You may, even at first glance, see certain imbalances of time usage that concern you. But there is no need to criticize it yet. To give your data a proper perspective, you will need to complete the Work Log, discussed below, and then step back—in the next chapter—to examine your individual needs and goals.

EXAMINING YOUR WORK WEEK

Unlike the above overall view of how you spend your total week, the Work Log examines exactly what you do at work. It needs to be precise to be valuable. For it, you will use

EXHIBIT 14.

Current Division of My Time

	Mon.	Tues.	Wed.	Thur.	Fri.	Sat.	Sun.
7:00 A.M.							
8:00 A.M.							
9:00 A.M.							
10:00 A.M.							
11:00 A.M.							
12:00 noon							
1:00 P.M.							
2:00 P.M.							
3:00 P.M.							
4:00 P.M.							

	Mon.	Tues.	Wed.	Thur.	Fri.	Sat.	Sun.
5:00 P.M.							
6:00 P.M.							
7:00 P.M.							
8:00 P.M.							
9:00 P.M.							
10:00 P.M.							
11:00 P.M.							
12:00 mid.							
1:00 A.M.							
2:00 A.M.							
3:00 A.M.							
4:00 A.M.							

	Mon.	Tues.	Wed.	Thur.	Fri.	Sat.	Sun.
5:00 A.M.							
6:00 A.M.							

Color Key:

☐ Work ☐ Sleep

☐ Family and social life

☐ Personal hobbies, recreation and interests

☐ Community, religious or charitable work

Exhibit 15. The purpose of this chart is to provide you with usable data not only on how you spend your time but also on the degree of control you have over that time usage. For this second purpose—analyzing the nature of the time you are spending at work—we are indebted to noted management authority Auren Uris. In his book, *The Efficient Executive*, Uris distinguishes among three kinds of work activity:

- *Fixed activity.* Uris defines this as "items in your work week that come up regularly and cannot be cut down." This would include such activities as staff meetings, production or sales figures reviews, routine approvals, and other administrative matters.

EXHIBIT 15

Work Log

Time	Task	F/S/V	Time	Task	F/S/V
Monday			**Tuesday**		
7:00 A.M.			7:00 A.M.		
7:30 A.M.			7:30 A.M.		
8:00 A.M.			8:00 A.M.		
8:30 A.M.			8:30 A.M.		
9:00 A.M.			9:00 A.M.		
9:30 A.M.			9:30 A.M.		
10:00 A.M.			10:00 A.M.		
10:30 A.M.			10:30 A.M.		
11:00 A.M.			11:00 A.M.		
11:30 A.M.			11:30 A.M.		
12:00 noon			12:00 noon		
12:30 P.M.			12:30 P.M.		

Time	Task	F/S/V	Time	Task	F/S/V
1:00 P.M.			1:00 P.M.		
1:30 P.M.			1:30 P.M.		
2:00 P.M.			2:00 P.M.		
2:30 P.M.			2:30 P.M.		
3:00 P.M.			3:00 P.M.		
3:30 P.M.			3:30 P.M.		
4:00 P.M.			4:00 P.M.		
4:30 P.M.			4:30 P.M.		
5:00 P.M.			5:00 P.M.		
5:30 P.M.			5:30 P.M.		
6:00 P.M.			6:00 P.M.		
6:30 P.M.			6:30 P.M.		
7:00 P.M.			7:00 P.M.		

Time	Task	F/S/V.	Time	Task	F/S/V
Wednesday			**Thursday**		
7:00 A.M.			7:00 A.M.		
7:30 A.M.			7:30 A.M.		
8:00 A.M.			8:00 A.M.		
8:30 A.M.			8:30 A.M.		
9:00 A.M.			9:00 A.M.		
9:30 A.M.			9:30 A.M.		
10:00 A.M.			10:00 A.M.		
10:30 A.M.			10:30 A.M.		
11:00 A.M.			11:00 A.M.		
11:30 A.M.			11:30 A.M.		
12:00 noon			12:00 noon		
12:30 P.M.			12:30 P.M.		

Time	Task	F/S/V	Time	Task	F/S/V
1:00 P.M.			1:00 P.M.		
1:30 P.M.			1:30 P.M.		
2:00 P.M.			2:00 P.M.		
2:30 P.M.			2:30 P.M.		
3:00 P.M.			3:00 P.M.		
3:30 P.M.			3:30 P.M.		
4:00 P.M.			4:00 P.M.		
4:30 P.M.			4:30 P.M.		
5:00 P.M.			5:00 P.M.		
5:30 P.M.			5:30 P.M.		
6:00 P.M.			6:00 P.M.		
6:30 P.M.			6:30 P.M.		
7:00 P.M.			7:00 P.M.		

Time Task	F/S/V	Week's Summary				
Friday		Day	Total No.Hrs. Worked	No. Hrs. Fixed	No.Hrs. Semi-flexible	No.Hrs. Variable
7:00 A.M.		**Mon.**				
7:30 A.M.		**Tues.**				
8:00 A.M.		**Wed.**				
8:30 A.M.		**Thurs.**				
9:00 A.M.		**Fri.**				
9:30 A.M.		Notes				
10:00 A.M.						
10:30 A.M.						
11:00 A.M.						
11:30 A.M.						
12:00 noon						
12:30 P.M.						

Time	Task	F/S/V	Week's Summary
1:00 P.M.			
1:30 P.M.			
2:00 P.M.			
2:30 P.M.			
3:00 P.M.			
3:30 P.M.			
4:00 P.M.			
4:30 P.M.			
5:00 P.M.			
5:30 P.M.			
6:00 P.M.			
6:30 P.M.			
7:00 P.M.			

- *Semiflexible activity.* This consists of "items which can be adjusted within limits." You may have to take care of these activities yourself—tasks such as handling routine correspondence, supervising your subordinates' work, meeting with suppliers or major customers—but they may not require the amount of time you are now allocating to each of them.

- *Variable activity.* Uris defines this as "those items that you can control completely." Such things might include attending business lunches, implementing ideas that you generate, making phone calls or visits, even attending to personal matters during office hours. For any of these activities, you have the option of choosing to eliminate them, choosing to expand them, or choosing some point in between.

Using Exhibit 15 should take little of your time. You might even choose to have your secretary keep the log. It is part of your secretary's job to keep track of your schedule, and so it will be routine for him or her to write down the tasks you perform as your day progresses. Only for a few moments at the end of each day will you be required to work on the chart—to judge the nature (fixed, semiflexible, variable) of each activity.

Here is how to use Exhibit 15:

- *Select a normal work week to study.* Perhaps no week in your job is like any other. For the purposes of Exhibit 15, all that you should do in choosing a week to study is to *avoid* one during which you know in advance that unique demands or crises will occur. Avoid, for example, selecting a week when you will be traveling— unless travel is a part of your regular routine.

• *Begin the morning of the week you choose by briefing your secretary.* First make copies of all six pages of Exhibit 15. (Again, as with Exhibit 14, you may wish to do this exercise again at a later date, so it is better not to use the original form in the book.) Then ask your secretary to jot down, half-hour by half-hour, what you are doing and with whom. It will be up to you, of course, to let the secretary know what you are doing, but remind him or her to ask you if you forget.

Each day's chart covers the period from 7:00 A.M. to 7:00 P.M., not because managers should put in twelve-hour days, but rather to allow for whatever flexibility there is in your schedule from day to day. The record should begin when you arrive at work each day, and it will end the moment you leave work. If you take work home with you, record the type of task and the amount of time you spend doing it on the line under 7:00 P.M..

For guidance, here are a few sample hours out of one manager's day:

11:30 A.M.	dictate letter; return Sam's call	S
NOON	lunch with Bill and Janet	V
12:30 P.M.	same	V
1:00 P.M.	weekly staff meeting	F
1:30 P.M.	same	F
2:00 P.M.	work on marketing report	S
2:30 P.M.	visit Jack, Mary, Tom	V
3:00 P.M.	make phone calls for Plough Co. account; read mail	S

- *At the end of each day, determine the nature of the time you spent.* In the F/S/V column next to each time slot, fill in the letter representing the appropriate category for the work you did—Fixed, Semiflexible, or Variable. Note the ways in which the manager cited above categorized those hours.

- *At the end of the week, summarize your findings.* In the Week's Summary of Exhibit 15, record the totals for each column heading for each day. Your secretary could do this for you. But doing it yourself can be beneficial, for you may start interpreting the figures as you review them.

    You may ask yourself several questions: Do I have more or less leeway in my time usage than I thought? How do I feel about the total number of hours I worked each day? What would I like to have spent more time on? What would I like to have eliminated? Jot down these thoughts in the Notes section. But again, as with Exhibit 14, at this point do not start making firm plans for change. Simply get an idea of the directions in which you would like to see changes made.

HOW WELL
DO YOU USE YOUR TIME?

The effectiveness of your own use of time depends on how closely *what* you do fits in with what you *want* to do—your own personal and professional needs and goals.

It is that correlation between aims and activities that many managers need to strengthen. In the Alexander Hamilton Institute survey of how top managers handle time, 82.4 percent of the respondents reported that they have explicitly stated goals and objectives for themselves. Yet, nearly 60 percent of these same managers also said that they wished to spend more time on family and social life, hobbies, recreation, and outside interests. Furthermore, 40 percent of the survey respondents felt they were spending too much time on work, while 20 percent wished to have more time.

DEVELOPING TIME-PLANNING TOOLS

To help you establish goals that are appropriate and achievable in your own particular circumstances, you will find Exhibit 16 extremely useful.

EXHIBIT 16

Self-Appraisal Worksheets

1. How much physical energy do I usually have?
   A lot_____   A moderate amount_____   Little_____

2. How frequently am I ill?
   Often_____   Occasionally_____   Seldom_____

3. How much intellectual energy do I usually have?
   A lot_____   A moderate amount_____   Little_____

4. How much emotional energy do I usually have?
   A lot_____   A moderate amount_____   Little_____

5. In what order are the five basic life activities important to me? (Rank them from 1 to 5, with 1 being most important.)

Work	_____	Hobbies, recreation, and interests	_____
Sleep	_____		
Family and social life	_____	Community, religious, or charitable work	_____

6. What activity did I rank highest in Question 5? _____
   What kinds of energy does this require?

	High	**Moderate**	**Low**
Physical	_____	_____	_____
Intellectual	_____	_____	_____
Emotional	_____	_____	_____

7. What activity did I rank second in Question 5? _____
   What kinds of energy does this require?

	High	**Moderate**	**Low**
Physical	_____	_____	_____
Intellectual	_____	_____	_____
Emotional	_____	_____	_____

8. What activity did I rank third in Question 5? _____
What kinds of energy does this require?

	High	**Moderate**	**Low**
Physical	_____	_____	_____
Intellectual	_____	_____	_____
Emotional	_____	_____	_____

9. How do the energy demands I checked in Questions 6 through 8 compare with my resources checked in Questions 1 through 4? Which demands can I easily meet? Which will require stretching my present resources?

_____

_____

_____

_____

_____

10. What activity did I rank highest in Question 5? _____
Which three specific facets of this activity do I like most? Which three do I like least?

_____

_____

_____

_____

_____

11. In the life activity I ranked highest in Question 5, what specific goals would I like to achieve in one year? In five years? In ten years?

_____

_____

_____

_____

_____

12. In the life activity I ranked highest in Question 5, what am I currently doing that I would like to stop doing by one year from now? By five years? By ten years?

_____

_____

_____

_____

_____

13. What activity did I rank second in Question 5? _____
What three specific facets of this activity do I like most? What three do I like least?

_____

_____

_____

_____

_____

14. In the life activity I ranked second in Question 5, what specific goals would I like to achieve in one year? In five years? In ten years?

_____

_____

_____

_____

_____

15. In the life activity I ranked second in Question 5, what am I currently doing that I would like to stop doing by one year from now? By five years? By ten years?

_____

_____

_____

_____

_____

16. What activity did I rank third in Question 5? _____
What three specific facets of this activity do I like most? What three do I like least?

_____

_____

_____

_____

_____

17. In the life activity I ranked third in Question 5, what specific goals would I like to achieve in one year? In five years? In ten years?

_____

_____

_____

_____

_____

_____

18. In the life activity I ranked third in Question 5, what am I currently doing that I would like to stop doing by one year from now? By five years? By ten years?

_____

_____

_____

_____

_____

_____

19. What external support will I need to achieve the goals I set in Question 11? (Think of such things as cooperation or agreement from specific people, financial or other material resources required.)

_____

_____

_____

_____

_____

_____

20. What external support will I need to achieve the goals I
set in Question 14?

_____

_____

_____

_____

_____

21. What external support will I need to achieve the goals I
set in Question 17?

_____

_____

_____

_____

_____

The data you generate from Exhibit 16 will provide a
foundation on which you can build the specific time-plan-
ning skills described in the next chapter.

The questions in this exercise appear relatively simple,
but the more genuine self-searching you do before answering
them, the closer you will come to an accurate profile of
yourself. Since this kind of serious thought requires concentration and uninterrupted time, we suggest that you take
the following measures to ensure the success of your effort:

- Set aside at least two hours to devote to this exercise.

- Select a time when you will not be interrupted.

- Choose a place where you will be comfortable, whether at home, at work, or at a neutral location such as a club or library.

- Answer the questions in pencil. The more you probe, the more you may wish to add or change. Use as much paper as you need; there is no need to confine your answers to the space we have provided.

HOW TO
USE YOUR TIME IN
THE WAY YOU WANT

Now that you have examined and defined the general directions you would like your life to take, you are ready to start thinking of ways to achieve those goals. Specifically, you have 168 hours each week as your basic resource. It will help to redefine your goals now in terms of activities to fill those 168 hours.

Exhibit 17, "Ideal Division of My Time," and Exhibit 18, "Ideal Work Log," are tools to help you in this redefinition. The patterns you create on these charts will serve as a personal challenge—both to inspire you and to prod you to work toward the achievement of your goals.

GUIDES TO ACHIEVING YOUR GOALS

Following are guides to filling out Exhibits 17 and 18. Subsequent chapters will help you turn your vision into a reality.

Exhibit 17 looks just like Exhibit 14, which you filled out earlier. The difference will lie in the meaning you give it. Here is how to fill it in:

- *Make a copy of the chart.* Even one's ideals can change with time and circumstances, and you may wish to do the exercise again at a later date.

- *Collect five writing instruments of different colors.* You can use pens, pencils, crayons, markers, or any combination thereof—as long as the marks are noticeably different from one another on paper.

- *Set aside a period of time to devote to filling out the chart.* This is an exercise you will have to concentrate on, and it is best to do it in one sitting.

- *Fill out the color key at the bottom of the page.* Use one writing instrument to symbolize each of the five basic life activities. Fill in each box with a different color.

- *Imagine a week over which you have total control.* If it helps, you can set an arbitrary future date on the week—say, six months from now, or one year or five years hence—but you do not have to date it at all. Simply eliminate from your vision of that week any external demands on your time. You are the initiator of all activities that will take place.

- *Begin with the life activity on which you would most like to spend more time.* Perhaps, for example, you wish to increase the time you spend on family and social life. If so, begin by filling in as many hours as you would really like to spend this way, in the appropriate color, during each day of the week.

EXHIBIT 17.

Ideal Division of My Time

	Mon.	Tues.	Wed.	Thurs.	Fri.	Sat.	Sun.
7:00 A.M.							
8:00 A.M.							
9:00 A.M.							
10:00 A.M.							
11:00 A.M.							
12:00 noon							
1:00 P.M.							
2:00 P.M.							
3:00 P.M.							
4:00 P.M.							

	Mon.	Tues.	Wed.	Thurs.	Fri.	Sat.	Sun.
5:00 P.M.							
6:00 P.M.							
7:00 P.M.							
8:00 P.M.							
9:00 P.M.							
10:00 P.M.							
11:00 P.M.							
12:00 mid.							
1:00 A.M.							
2:00 A.M.							
3:00 A.M.							
4:00 A.M.							

	Mon.	Tues.	Wed.	Thurs.	Fri.	Sat.	Sun.
5:00 A.M.							
6:00 A.M.							

Color Key:

☐ Work   ☐ Sleep   ☐ Family and social life

☐ Hobbies, recreation and interests

☐ Community, religious, or charitable work

- *Go on to your next most valued activity.* Perhaps you would like to put in a specific number of extra hours, some days, on work. Continue by filling in those hours in their appropriate color.

- *Continue, in order of their importance to you, with the remaining three activities.* Color in the hours you would like to spend on each, in its appropriate color. It is possible that you will choose entirely to eliminate one activity—perhaps, for example, you will eliminate work if you are planning to retire; or you might feel that you have done your share of community work and wish to end your involvement.

The color patterns of this completed chart will show you how you would like your week to look. At this point, you might want to go back to Exhibit 14 and see the differences between your real life and the life you consider ideal.

You might also now think of talking to other people (with or without showing them the charts) about the changes you are planning for your life. Perhaps a close friend would be best to talk to, or your spouse or another family member. Perhaps even someone at work or in one of the organizations you belong to.

The advantage of finding a sympathetic person to share your goals with is twofold: the other person may be able to make it easier for you to do what you wish; and you will feel more firmly committed to your plan after you have in some small way made it "public" by confiding in someone else.

YOUR IDEAL WORK LOG

Exhibit 18 will be the work schedule you would like to have. We begin, as we did in Exhibit 17, by assuming that you have complete control over your time—that you are free to do what you choose for as long as you choose. And so, instead of dividing your time according to the nature of the demands on it, as we did in Exhibit 15, here we will divide it according to the actual functions with which you wish to fill it.

Here is how to use Exhibit 18:

• *Reserve a period of uninterrupted time.* It will probably take at least an hour to do the analysis properly. You will need freedom to concentrate without being interrupted.

EXHIBIT 18

Ideal Work Log

Work Functions	Mon.	Tues.	Wed.	Thurs.	Fri.
1.					
2.					
3.					
4.					
5.					
6.					
7.					
8.					
9.					
10.					
11.					
12.					
13.					
14.					
15.					
16.					
Total Hours Worked					

- *Fill in the Work Functions column in pencil.* Work functions are such things as administrative routines; meetings with subordinates; dealing with clients or suppliers; dealings with industry, trade, or government regulatory agencies or associations; long-range planning; budgeting; research; public relations; employee relations; on-the-job socializing; and so on. List in that column each function you wish to do. You may be performing some of these functions now. Others may be tasks you would like to perform. Do not include any of your present chores that you do not wish to continue. Complete this list in pencil, for the longer you think about it, the more changes you may wish to make. Include as many or as few functions as you think would be ideal.

- *Fill in total number of hours worked each day.* This is information you may want to carry over from Exhibit 17. Perhaps, for example, you would like to work five eight-hour days each week. Or maybe you would like to take a day or an afternoon off each week. For each day, set down the number of hours you would like to spend at work.

- *Allocate your work functions among the hours you have planned.* Perhaps you would, for example, like to spend one hour a day, three days a week, on administrative matters. Or maybe you would like to devote an hour a day to working with your subordinates. Or perhaps you would like to reserve a three-hour period each week for research. Take the total time you are willing to work, and divide it into periods of time for each function you wish to perform.

This completed chart is your blueprint for the future. The closer you can come to spending your days as the chart describes, the more effectively you will be using your own time and talents. While you may not accomplish your time allocations overnight, the chapters that follow can help steer you firmly in the desired direction.

18

HOW YOU
CAN ACHIEVE YOUR IDEAL
TIME USAGE

If you have gone through the self-analyses in the preceding chapters, you have undoubtedly had several insights into your own uniqueness. Some of these insights may have been pleasant ones that brought to the surface your long-buried dreams or aspirations, or helped you understand your own contradictory types of behavior. Other insights may have been painful, in that they revealed wasted opportunities or foretold changes in the routine with which you have become comfortable. The insights you have gained about yourself, and about how you wish to spend your time, will serve as a blueprint for effectively using your own time. This self-information defines what you have, what you lack and want, what you have and don't want—all to do with your time.

But you need more than a blueprint if you intend to build a house, and you will need to go beyond self-analysis if you wish to improve your use of time. You need the skills and methods discussed below to realize your potential. Now that you know what you want, you must develop the skills that will help you get it.

LEARNING TO TAKE RESPONSIBILITY
FOR YOUR TIME AND CHOICES

Assuming responsibility for yourself means making conscious decisions about what you are doing and then fully accepting the consequences of those decisions—good or bad. Every manager knows and uses this process for making business decisions, but few extend it to other facets of their lives. Here are some things that can help accustom you to thinking in these terms for everything:

- *In speech and writing, abandon the passive for the active voice.* The way you speak reveals your thought patterns. The passive "It happened" is a very different thought from "I made it happen." "It was decided" is a foggy way of saying "I decided."

- *Start saying "I want" unaggressively.* Many people state the simple, direct truth that they want something only as a last resort, and then they say it in anger because it is a last resort. Try starting out with "I want" instead of the manipulative "Wouldn't you like..." or the authoritarian "You should..." or the evasive "They want me to ask you...."

  Not everything you ask of people is an expression of your personal desire. The nature of your work creates demands that must be met. But, as a leader, you are often responsible for choosing how to meet those demands. Why not be open about that? Away from work, even the most outspoken manager is often hesitant to say "I want" for fear of rejection. But the better you become at saying honestly what you want, the greater your chances will be of getting it.

- *Empower yourself to reach your own goals.* In your job, you are constantly aware of the full range of your formal powers, and you take responsibility for your actions. Start accepting equally your informal powers in every aspect of your life. State your wishes, even if you think they'll never be granted, and start allowing yourself to seek ways of getting what you want. Both "I can" and "I can't" can be self-fulfilling prophecies; so why not try "I can"?

- *See consequences as what they really are.* When you fail, you must understand that you failed at one particular task—and only at that. Don't magnify a failure and allow it to reflect on unrelated areas of your life. And, great as the temptation is to see a success as larger than it is, resist that, too. "I did this well" can give you a good feeling that may carry over to something else; but extrapolating—"I am good at everything"—from unrelated successes just sets you up for failure.

ESTABLISHING CLEAR PRIORITIES

Some time-management experts claim that arranging things according to their degree of importance to you is the only step necessary for taking charge of your time. But most people cannot keep themselves rigidly programmed for very long, no matter how logical their schedule may be.

We will start with the assumption that the most effective way to establish priorities is to make them clear and simple enough to be adaptable to your various moods, activities, and circumstances. The work that you have already done in defining your own needs and goals should be the basis for setting your own priorities. Here are some guidelines to help you get started:

- *Priorities are levels of relative value.* One thing alone cannot have a priority; its relative value can be determined only by weighing it against something else.

- *Relative value is subjective.* What is of value to you is determined by your own unique mix of intelligence, experience, desires, and talents. Just because something is generally accepted as valuable does not necessarily mean that it is appropriate for you. For instance, some managers shun the corner offices that others covet; some highly educated people prefer to go to the movies rather than to the opera.

  The converse, of course, is equally true: just because something is generally held in low regard does not necessarily mean that it has little value to you. Many people prefer mixed-breed dogs to pure-breds; others are bored by golf and really enjoy tennis.

- *Since your time is limited, you have to make choices about what is worth spending time on.* Like any other precious resource, time requires careful management if you are to derive maximum value from it.

- *To define your highest priorities, look back at the charts you have filled out.* Note the discrepancies between your present time allocation and the ideal you would like to achieve. Determine the discrepancies you would most like to correct, *not* the ones that would be fastest or easiest to correct. Select the three or four ways of using time that are of most value to you.

- *Make these three or four changes your continuing goals.* Once you have chosen the three or four areas of change that would most enhance the value you derive from your time, concentrate on them. Phrase them to yourself in simple sentences starting with "I want." Repeat these sentences to yourself at least several times a day. Do not dissipate this energy by thoughts of other, less important changes. These sentences represent your high priority goals; make them an active part of your consciousness.

EFFECTIVE PLANNING

Focusing clearly on your goals is the first step to realizing them. The next step is to make specific plans. The only effective plans are enforceable ones. So you must avoid trying to structure your life in such a way that the structure itself becomes a burden, defeating the basic purpose of the changes you have chosen to make. Here are some basic methods of effective, goal-oriented planning:

• *Schedule your time as loosely as possible.* Certainly, each day and week there will be some activities that have to be planned for specific times. Usually these are contacts with other people such as business, community, or social meetings or other gatherings. Accept the fact that some of these are necessarily committed blocks of time, but keep free as much of the rest of your time as possible. Free time is not to be thought of as wasted time; it is time for which you are free to determine the most effective use.

• *Where possible, schedule necessary commitments at times convenient for you.* The object of planning your time is to leave large periods of time uncommitted, and thus available for your choice of activities. To do that, you must schedule your meetings and other obligations so that they do not leave small pieces of minimally usable time around them. Plan meetings, for example, first thing in the morning, or right before lunch, or directly after you leave work.

- *Plan ahead for what you will need from others.* If your own projects or activities require contributions from others, get those contributions before you begin to invest your own time on the projects. Give deadlines to other people for materials or information you know you will need. With these in hand, you will not be stymied by the lack of some element essential to your own completion of the task.

- *Keep the things you need where you can find them easily.* You do not have to be a model of neatness or organization to keep your things in order. Order simply means knowing where things are. It takes only a small effort to put something back where it belongs after you have used it.

- *Recognize the link between activities and goals.* You know now what your goals are—and what their priorities are. As you go from one activity to another, ask yourself what larger goal each activity is leading you to, or diverting you from reaching. If one of your goals, for example, is spending more time alone on a hobby, you may see more clearly the need to decline an offer to chair a committee for a charity group you belong to. But if one of your goals is to devote more of yourself to that charity, you would accept the offer and perhaps delegate to someone else in your company your place on a committee investigating new marketing approaches for your firm's products. Seen in relation to your goals, each activity you involve yourself in will clearly assume its proper degree of importance to you. Once you recognize that degree of importance, you can act accordingly.

WORKING WITH YOUR
INTRINSIC ENERGY PATTERNS

Your own energy—physical, emotional, and intellectual—is the basic raw material of your life. It determines how well you use your time. We envy those who seem to have boundless energy. It is true that some people are healthier, need less sleep, and can sustain activity longer than others. But it is also true that few of us have learned to make the best use of the raw energy we do have.

Here are some ways in which you can exploit your energy to its full potential:

- *Develop healthful habits.* It is still true that eating nutritiously, getting an adequate amount of sleep, exercising regularly, and avoiding the overuse of tobacco, alcohol, and other drugs is the key to physical well-being.

- *Recognize your own patterns.* Charting one's own biorhythms has become something of a fad. You don't really need any elaborate system or equipment to know how you feel and what you feel like doing. Once you strip your calendar of unproductive activities, you will be free to do what you are best able to do with most of your time.

  Start tuning in to the signals of your body and mind. Perhaps you think better early in the day. If so, that's when you should do things that require concentration. Or perhaps you work better as the day progresses. Then it might be useful to stay up later, get up later, and start the day with tasks that are physically rather than intellectually demanding, such as inspecting factory operations or traveling. There are days when your emotional energy level is high. Those are the times to interview people, have important discussions with colleagues and subordinates, return phone calls, and so on. When you have a "down" day, don't try to ignore it. Select activities that minimize interpersonal stress. The better you gear your activities to your own present state, the more effectively you will be using your time, and the better you will feel.

- *Think of what your activities demand of you.* Certainly, your first thought about any given activity is what its results will be—in other words, how it will fit in with your goals. But the second thought is just as necessary—what it will require of you. Some tasks, such as ordinary correspondence, are fairly routine and require only patience. Others, such as writing a speech, are innovative and demand creativity. Still others, like chairing a large meeting, require physical stamina or, like budget preparation, demand detailed concentration. The more you think in terms of which energies will be called upon by a task, the better you will be able to fit the task to your own best time to do it.

- *Make your habits flexible.* All personal habits start out as energy savers. If you routinely brush your teeth before you shower in the morning, that habit saves you the trouble of having to make a daily decision. If you routinely go through your mail first thing each morning because it helps you ease into the business day, that habit saves having to think about it more than once. As long as a habit is still fulfilling a purpose you want, it is serving you.

     But, over time, both you and the circumstances of your life change. With change, old habits often become masters rather than servants. For example, one manager always got up in the morning a half-hour earlier than necessary in order to read the newspaper before leaving for work. That habit began years before when she drove a car to work. But now she takes the train, and is frequently tired. She could get an extra half-hour of sleep each morning by reading the paper on the train.

Since habits are things you do almost automatically, you may have to rethink their value. But it is worth the effort not to let anything you do become so firmly a part of your life that it outlasts its usefulness to you.

DEVELOPING TRUST IN OTHER PEOPLE

Management is the art of getting things done by other people—that is one definition of the manager's job. Yet your entire life, not just your work, depends on getting results from other people.

Your community or charitable work requires many of the same interpersonal skills you use in your job. Even within your family, group goals are never accomplished solely by one individual. Since so much of what you want to achieve depends on the efforts of others, you can enhance your effectiveness by developing productive relationships. At work or off the job, with colleagues, friends, or family members, you can use these guidelines to help you depend on other people without abdicating responsibility for your own life:

- *Select your helpers carefully.* The people you can trust most are those who share your goals or for whom you feel an attraction. This does not necessarily mean that those you can trust most are most like you. In fact, the most productive relationships are usually based on complementary qualities rather than similar ones.

- *Recognize the other person as a complete human being*. The more completely people understand each other, the more effective their working relationship will be. For example, most managers prefer to work with a private secretary rather than with the stenographic pool, even for the most routine tasks. They feel more confident that the work will be done right by someone they know personally. Of course, the more complex the task the more important it becomes to know the experience, the personal goals, the temperament, the unique skills and capabilities, even the weaknesses of those to be entrusted with it.

- *Reveal as much of yourself as you can with the people you will have to trust*. It makes sense for people who are working for you to know as much about you as practicable. It helps them understand more deeply exactly what you want and why. Reveal your goals, your objectives, your relevant preferences. The stronger the foundation you give them for understanding the purpose of what is to be done, the more autonomously they will be able to do it. If they can carry out the task without supervision, they will derive more satisfaction from it, and you can feel confident about entrusting it to them.

- *Delegate as much work as possible*. The more tasks you delegate to others, the more fully you are communicating your trust. Most people will respond to your trust by being trustworthy. So delegate not just a task, but also the responsibility for meeting a goal. The more choices you leave to the other person, the richer the assignment will seem to its recipient and the lighter your burden will be.

- *Make status reports a part of the tasks you delegate.*
Many managers are uneasy about delegation because
they fear not knowing what is going on. You can eliminate that concern by setting up times when people will
provide you with status reports.

    When you make an assignment, ask for a written
or oral report of interim results at a certain time. Then
you won't have to wonder how the job is going. The
same principle applies to jobs you are sharing with
someone else, such as fund-raising for the local hospital.
Establish times to share results to date and discuss problems that might have arisen. This helps avoid crises,
which are unproductive and disruptive.

- *Be at least as free with praise as you are with criticism.*
Praise is not only a reward but also a reminder to people
of what the standards are, so they can continue to aim
for them the next time. Certainly, when something goes
wrong, you must clear it up. But just as certainly when
things go right, you should express your satisfaction.
Praise people specifically for what they have done: "Bill,
I am delighted that you beat the production schedule by
forty-eight hours."

LEARNING TO SAY NO

If you are to do what you want with your time, you must
learn *not* to do what you *don't* want. The following guidelines can help you sort out—and appropriately handle—
the various demands on your time:

- *Say yes immediately only to requests that promise to
advance your own goals.* If you are determined to become more active in trade or professional associations,

you might immediately accept an invitation to speak at such a meeting. Saying yes to such worthwhile requests will force you to make time for them. It will also encourage the people you want to spend more time with to continue to seek you out.

- *Say no to requests that run counter to your goals.* Suppose, for example, that you want to spend more time on personal interests or with your family. If so, you might be flattered when you are invited to represent your firm on a goodwill business trip abroad, but you should decline it immediately. You may even find that both you and your firm will benefit by letting an able and ambitious subordinate shoulder the responsibility in your stead. Even in smaller matters, such as attending routine meetings, quasi-social business dinners, or an evening out doing something you don't care for, a prompt "no, thank you" will allow you to avoid wasting time and energy.

- *Delay your decisions on all other requests.* When you are not certain how you feel about a request for your time, allow yourself to delay your decision. Say that you don't know, that you will decide later. Then, when you are not under direct and immediate pressure, weigh the matter, even if it is a small one. Ask yourself these five questions:

1. Would I enjoy doing this?

2. How would I benefit personally or professionally from doing this?

3. How important is this to people who are important to me?

4. Will this keep me from doing something else that is important to me?

5. If I don't do this, what will be the consequences? Are they serious threats to the achievement of my own goals?

- By asking yourself these questions, you will be able to distinguish between those requests that are worthy of a yes and those that deserve a no. To make the best use of your time, you should make reasoned decisions about *all* requests for your time for a week or two. After a while, such mental sorting will become automatic.

- *Learn to say no without offending people.* When someone requests your time, that person is paying you a compliment. This is why it is often so difficult to deny such requests. Sometimes you can soften your refusal by suggesting an alternative—for example, another person who could do it instead. When your answer must be a simple no, do not try to dilute it with apologies or excuses. Say, "I am sorry, but I cannot do it," or "Thank you for asking me, but I must say no." If the other person persists, simply repeat your no calmly and without anger or annoyance. After all, your goal here is to decline the invitation, not to offend the other person.

MAKING TIME FOR YOURSELF ALONE

Experts estimate that managers spend about 80 percent of their time dealing directly with other people. Off the job, most managers are also surrounded by people—family, friends, colleagues, neighbors, and so on. Most of these contacts are pleasant or necessary to the manager's total life, but they also demand energy that needs regular replenishment. A good night's sleep is not enough. And neither is the time you spend alone at your desk working on specific tasks. You need solitary free time to absorb and digest the constant bombardment of information and to make sense out of and give order to the events of your life. There are several ways of making such time for yourself:

- *Schedule "quiet hours" at work.* Many managers contrive to spend either the first or the last hour of each day alone, with instructions that they are not to be disturbed. If the only way you can relax is to create time tc do so, this method might be best for you.

- *Take advantage of natural breaks.* If you are flexible by nature, you may find it possible to take small pieces of free time here and there to isolate yourself for ten to fifteen minutes and just relax.

- *Enjoy the isolation of commuting.* Some managers take advantage of their time in a commuter bus, train, or car to organize their day's activities, or go through old mail, or get other kinds of work done. If you use your travel time for work, this may not be the right time to relax, but it is worth considering if the work could be better done elsewhere.

- *Reserve a set time to be alone at home.* If you are an early riser, you might spend the hour before breakfast by yourself. Or, if it fits into your family schedule, you could isolate yourself for a half-hour after work.

- *Take up solitary activities at home.* Some managers involve themselves in relaxing activities that help free their minds. Gardening, listening to music, woodworking, or other crafts can serve this purpose.

- *Learn to relax.* Some individuals find meditation an effective way to still the mental turmoil of a busy life. Others relax their minds by occupying their hands with physical work of one sort or another. Still others relax mentally by exercising. And some simply sit quietly and allow their thoughts free rein.

Remember that at work, on the road, or at home, this time is for your own recreation or rejuvenation. You may find that the time alone produces constructive ideas or solutions to problems you are facing. But do not burden yourself with specific goals for this time, or it will not provide the relaxation you need.

STAYING IN THE PRESENT

"Real time"—for people as well as computers—means right now. The only real time is the present; the past and future are constructions of the sophisticated human mind. The ideas of "before now" and "after now" do, of course, have great value and are uniquely human. But, in terms of making the most of your time, they are hindrances. The key to using your time most effectively is to take full advantage of each moment you have. You can do that only by devoting yourself to the moment, in the moment. Here are some guidelines to doing it:

- *Accept responsibility for your choices.* At each moment, whatever you are doing, you have chosen to do it. No one has forced you into it. If you have chosen unwisely, you have the choice of changing. If you have chosen well, you are responsible for doing the best you can.

- *Regard each choice positively.* You have chosen to spend an hour on something. So devote the hour to it. Do not dilute your energy by indulging in doubts—concerns about other things you are not doing, or will be doing at some later time.

- *If something keeps bothering you, deal with it.* Every now and then, a problem can become obsessive, intruding on time and energy meant for other tasks. Even if it is relatively unimportant to your actual goals, a problem such as plans for a meeting or writing a difficult letter or keeping a long-postponed promise must be dealt with if you are to free your mind. The most constructive action, of course, is to do it and get it over with if you possibly can. If you cannot take care of the problem now, plan a definite time when you will do so. Knowing you are thus committed will help keep that problem from blocking your attention to the tasks at hand now.

- *From time to time each day, consciously recognize the moment you have.* Just for a split second, perhaps five or six times each day, jolt yourself to a halt and look around. Recognize that "This is where I am, and this is what I am doing." This simple exercise helps keep you centered, in balance, and attuned to your own unique "now." People who stop periodically to take stock of the moment find that their concentration on the matter at hand is heightened and so is their effectiveness in dealing with it.

HOW TO
CONTROL THE FOUR BIG
TIME CONSUMERS

The key elements in every managerial job are other people. They make success possible. They also, quite often, ruin the best laid plans for your time. In-person interruptions, meetings, telephone calls, and requests for information are, in that order, the biggest challenges to time management.

CONTROLLING IN-PERSON
INTERRUPTIONS

Obviously, when something critical comes up suddenly, you will want to be interrupted. But non-urgent and casual interruptions of one kind or another reduce your effectiveness as a manager.

There are two ways to limit interruptions. First, you can withdraw. Simply make yourself unavailable except at certain times each day. Second, you can be available, but take certain steps to ensure that the interruptions are valid ones. Few managers always follow one course or the other. Most find that some combination of the two methods is best.

Following are guidelines to implement each strategy. You will find the best path for you by choosing those guidelines most relevant to your own personality and responsibilities.

Withdrawing

Certainly, no manager wishes to be totally isolated from informal contact with others. But some people need more privacy than others, and some tasks require more single-minded attention than others do. Here are some strategies for withdrawing when necessary:

- *Reserve "quiet time."* Arriving at the office early or asking your secretary to allow no interruptions for a given time will ensure your isolation.

- *Reserve "people time."* Set aside an hour or two each day during which time you will be available to people who want to chat. If people come by at other times, your secretary can tell them when you will be ready to see them. Your colleagues and subordinates will soon understand and will arrange their casual visits at your convenience.

- *Find "quiet space."* You may find that your own office is sufficiently isolated to serve as a retreat. If not, or if you need extended private time, find a remote vacant office, a corporate library, or an unused conference room to work in. Only your secretary needs to know your whereabouts in case of emergencies.

- *Make your schedule formal.* The ultimate enemy of casual interruption is a tight calendar. If you really wish to eliminate surprise visits, the best way to do so is to see no one without an appointment arranged through your secretary. He or she can make appointments for you according to your own guidelines. You will decide whom you will see, about what, and for how long. Your secretary can enforce time limits for you by notifying your visitors of the length of their appointments, interrupting you, if necessary, to make sure visitors do not stay too long.

Being Available When Needed

Most managers recognize the benefits of casual visits from others in the organization. When your door is open, literally or figuratively, that helps create a certain climate for the firm that many leaders value. Being casually available to people also can help you stay in touch with the life currents of the organization. Rich as these benefits are, however, you must weigh them against the danger that your own priorities will suffer from too much time leakage each day. You can use these strategies to achieve the proper balance you need:

- *Delegate effectively.* When people who work for you are uncertain of the limits of their authority or responsibility, they will come back to you frequently. To avoid these unproductive interruptions, eliminate their cause. Give subordinates as much control over their work as possible. And, when colleagues come to you with matters others can handle for you, refer them to those individuals.

- *Meet subordinates at their place of work.* When someone asks to see you about something briefly, you can better control the time it takes if you are the visitor rather than the host. In your own office, unless you arrange to have your secretary interrupt you at a certain time, it will be difficult for you to end the discussion. But if you are somewhere else, you can simply excuse yourself and leave whenever you wish.

- *Get around regularly.* The more you visit others when it is convenient for you, the less need people will feel to interrupt you when you are working. To this end, many managers make a point of moving around to chat with colleagues and subordinates as a regular part of each work week.

- *Protect yourself from nuisance callers.* Even the most sociable and open managers question the value of being available when a few people regularly take advantage of it by prolonged time-wasting sessions. Be selective. Your secretary can act as filter by steering the nuisances away. You, too, can discourage them individually by refusing them time or severely limiting the time you do offer them. This individualized treatment will still keep you open to visits from more welcome members of the company.

- *Be open about your own preferences.* People have no way of knowing what talk you value and what you don't, unless you tell them. If someone comes to you with a matter of no interest or meaning to you, simply say, "I'm sorry, John, but this really isn't in my area of the business." Change the subject or end the discussion. It is even more important to show your appreciation when people come to you with matters you do want to hear about. Comments like "I am very glad we talked about this" or "Thank you very much for letting me know" will let people know what kinds of things you are open to discuss.

GETTING MAXIMUM BENEFITS FROM MEETINGS

Meetings are at once the crux and the bane of a manager's work life. When they are successful, meetings bring forth creative ideas, solve problems, and provide opportunities for efficient communication. They give participants a sense of accomplishment and satisfaction. When meetings are unsuccessful, however, they are sources of anger, frustration, and resentment at the unproductive use of precious time.

The complex human interactions that take place at meetings are various. The checklist in Exhibit 19 can help you make sure that the meetings you attend will be worth the time you spend on them. Try using the checklist before your next meeting, adding questions that apply to that particular situation. Your answers will provide guidelines for appropriate action. Then use it regularly; the more often you use it, the more valuable questions of your own you will be able to add, and the more firmly you can decide how to handle each meeting.

TAMING THE TELEPHONE

The telephone is often used for purposes that could be more effectively served by other means. Such misuse makes it a potential enemy to effective utilization of time. If you follow the DO's and DON'Ts of telephone usage below, you will avoid the pitfalls and reap the benefits the telephone makes possible. The same guidelines hold for calls you make and calls you accept from other people.

- *DO use the telephone to save steps or travel.*

EXHIBIT 19

Increasing the Productivity of Meetings

YES	NO	
_____	_____	Do I want to attend this meeting?
_____	_____	Does it promise to help me in any way to come closer to any of my own goals?
_____	_____	Could someone else take my place at this meeting, representing my interests and reporting back results?
_____	_____	Is this an opportunity to expand the horizons of a promising subordinate?
_____	_____	Do I feel that the people scheduled to participate in the meeting are all necessary to the purpose of the group?
_____	_____	Is there anyone not invited to the meeting who could be of genuine value to the group?
_____	_____	Is the purpose of meeting clearly defined?
_____	_____	Do all participants know in advance what results the group is expected to achieve?
_____	_____	Am I aware of any purpose to the meeting that does not appear on its agenda? (Power struggles to be resolved, for example, or favorite ideas to be squeezed in?)
_____	_____	Is there a better means of taking care of the business at hand—by memo, for example?
_____	_____	Do I know exactly what I wish to gain by going to this meeting?
_____	_____	Are there alternative ways by which I can achieve my purposes?
_____	_____	What would I do with this time if I were not going to the meeting?

- *DO use the telephone to gather information you need immediately*. A quick call to verify a figure, a date, or a name is the best way to meet a momentary need. It is also a valuable way to get a quick opinion from someone whose expertise you value.

- *DO use the telephone to disseminate information immediately*. When you must notify someone quickly of a decision you have made or something you have learned, the telephone is the best way to do it.

- *DO use the telephone to set up last-minute appointments or meetings*. Calling is an informal and effective way of coordinating schedules to get people together.

- *DO use the telephone for progress reports on important ongoing activities*. When a subordinate is handling an emergency, for example, the wise manager asks him or her to phone in whenever possible. Or when you are away from your office, the phone helps you keep in touch with what is going on in your absence.

- *DO use the telephone to stay in touch with business associates, customers, and other key people*.

- *DO use the telephone for simple group decision-making*. No need to call a meeting for routine matters that require the simple agreement of several other people. Just call and ask for okays. Only if problems arise in these calls would a meeting be appropriate.

- *DO use the telephone if it gives you a good feeling*. Many managers use the telephone for matters that really do not require its use simply because they like to. If this is your preference, use it generously. But if you regard the phone as a necessary evil, then scrupulously limit your telephone calls.

- *DON'T use the telephone in place of a formal business letter*. Any important agreements or decisions will eventually have to be put in writing. You may as well do so at once and save a call.

- *DON'T use the telephone when a memo could do the job*. Unless the topic is sensitive, anything you have to tell three or more people is better dictated by you once than reiterated on the phone many times.

- *DON'T use the telephone for delicate discussions*. Authorities tell us that an enormous amount of information is conveyed by body attitudes and facial expressions. These are absent over the telephone, and their loss can be critical to the effectiveness of what you have to say. Disciplining a subordinate, investigating a troublesome rumor, and sounding someone out before a big change require face-to-face communication.

- *DON'T use the telephone for non-urgent one-way messages*. If you simply want to tell someone something and time is not critical, just dictate a memo or letter.

- *DON'T use the telephone to discuss lengthy, complex matters unless a face-to-face meeting is impossible*. One's span of attention is shorter on the phone than in person, and you have little control over the distractions around the person you are talking to.

GETTING INFORMATION

Managers constantly need all kinds of information, and they often have trouble getting it. There is, of course, no way of ensuring that you will always know or have access to every piece of information that might be helpful to you. But there are several ways you can spread your information net widely:

- *Learn your secretary's secrets.* It can help you to know how and where your regular files are kept, where and by what codes addresses and phone numbers are filed, what is done with computer printouts after you have seen them. You may need to find something fast when your secretary is away or busy.

- *Tell your secretary what's on your mind.* This is a generally good practice to make the two of you a smooth-running team. It can also be valuable for you to know your secretary's thoughts about what you are doing. A secretary may know things about people and work in the organization that can be useful to you. Yet it might not occur to your assistant to share this lore unless you show an open mind.

- *Keep your subordinates apprised of your projects.* They, too, may have useful information that they will share when they know of your interest.

- *Learn as much as you can about your computer's capabilities.* Your company's data processing people might be able to do more for you if they know what your needs are. Talk to your data processing manager to find out how much more useful that department could be in providing you with the facts and figures you need.

- *Recognize the informal leaders below you.* Regardless of their position in the formal organization chart, some people are information gatherers or informal leaders. Perhaps because they are curious, or because they inspire the confidence of others, or simply because their work puts them in contact with many members of the organization, these people know much more than the average person about the people and work of the company. The wise manager stays in close touch with such subordinates and is well informed as a result.

A TEN-POINT
PLAN FOR MANAGING
YOUR TIME

This concluding section distills the key points made earlier and provides a practical tool for helping you change your time-use patterns. While you may wish to review various sections of this book periodically and to rework some of the self-analysis tools, this section is designed to become an integral part of your daily life. By following these ten steps, by using them to plan and organize your time, you will be able to change and grow in the directions you desire.

1. *Keep a small notebook with you.* A pocket- or purse-size appointment calendar is excellent for this purpose. A miniature spiral-bound or loose-leaf notebook would also be useful. Here you can write down your goals, activities, and even your random ideas. If you balk at the idea of putting such things in writing, remember that it takes discipline to set goals and work toward their fulfillment. Formalizing your goals and your plans by putting them in writing will heighten your commitment to carrying them out.

How you actually organize your notebook is as individual a matter as its contents. The structure should make sense to you, and should allow both ease of entry and ease of retrieval of the data you record. You might want to use a page a day, a page a week, or a page a month, with separate pages devoted to goals and ideas. Or you may wish to organize your notebook on a goal-by-goal basis, with the calendar part simply for reference. You may want to incorporate a detailed list of activities for each day or week. And you might reserve a section for facts, figures, names, phone numbers, or other data you frequently need. The more concisely you can organize the purposes to which you wish to assign your time, the freer you will be to act in accordance with those purposes.

2. *Plan your goals on a monthly basis.* For most people, any longer time span than a month becomes too vague to deal with. Also, for most goals, any shorter time span than a month is not sufficient to show progress.

3. *Set only the goals you genuinely desire to achieve.* If you set goals contrary to your true inclinations, you are courting failure. When you fail to meet these goals, your sense of failure (or guilt) will hinder you from achieving the goals you genuinely desire.

   Do set goals you want to achieve even if you doubt your ability to meet them. If you deeply want something, allowing that desire to surface will help you find a means to succeed eventually—or will at least point you in directions that are right for you and that you might otherwise not have seen. Each month, as you plan your goals, the changes you have made in your life the month before will help you chart your course.

4. *Evaluate results on a monthly basis.* At the end of each month, see how much closer you have come to reaching your goals. But remember that this is not a competition, that you are not being judged or graded on your results. Change, in time usage and in life direction, needs time and space to occur and take hold.

Do not be too excited by spectacular success in one month. And, similarly, do not be discouraged if one month shows negligible results or even some backsliding. If you begin to doubt the appropriateness of your chosen aims, return to the charts in this book. Look over what you have written about yourself and, if necessary, rework the exercises to bring your purposes up-to-date.

5. *Plan a few specific goal-related activities on a day-to-day basis.* Right now, your days are too full. Routine demands will continue. So, to make any changes in the use of your time, you will have to make a conscious effort to do some things you are not doing now.

Start each day with the determination to include one or two activities that relate to one or more of your goals. They may be small things, like writing a letter or making a phone call to get information or to establish a new contact. Or they may be more ambitious, such as seeking an invitation to speak to an organization you wish to become involved in. But make these activities your first priorities for the day. If you insist on achieving them, you will begin to see what other tasks can be eliminated or compressed into less time.

6. *Make time-usage evaluation an integral part of each new activity.* Until it becomes habit, make a conscious effort to step back a moment before you begin each new task or enter each new situation. Ask yourself whether it really needs doing, why you are the one to do it, and

what benefits you expect to reap from your investment of time in it.

You and others make certain demands on your time each day. Many of these are so routine that you respond to them almost automatically. As a result, you may not be making the wisest use of your time. When you examine what you are doing, you will find some things that have no link to what you wish to accomplish. As you recognize these, choose to do something else with that time.

You will find that some of your activities are taking up amounts of time disproportionate to their importance. As you recognize these, you will devise ways to streamline them. And you will also find some activities worthy of more time than you have heretofore offered them. By revising your time allocations, you will make that time available.

7. *Use the clock sparingly*. When you chat with a colleague about a matter of concern to you both, you cannot know how many minutes the talk will require to meet a suitable end. And when you arbitrarily limit the time you will spend writing a critical report, you may force yourself to cut short a highly productive train of thought. To be most effective you must allow for spontaneity. You need the freedom to pursue a thought, or task, or conversation for however long it takes to reap its potential worth.

Begin to loosen up your schedule. Make fewer firm time commitments each day and respond to the exigencies of each matter. If you schedule an hour-long meeting, and the task is completed in forty mintues, end the meeting immediately. If you intend to confer briefly with a colleague about a matter of minor importance, and spontaneously the talk goes to a vital, larger matter, stay as long as the conversation is productive. If your mind is just not working well with figures at the moment, put your budget aside and spend your time more usefully on something else. Don't try to force yourself into a concentration you cannot muster at this moment.

8. *Recognize the value of each moment.* Each moment has its own opportunities and limitations. The sooner you recognize the value of the present, the better you will be able to exploit its possibilities and avoid its pitfalls. Become aware of how you feel now—physically, mentally, emotionally. Become aware of your environment—the light, the space, the physical objects around you, and the people you work with.

9. *Start to use that value fully.* You know what you want. And you have become aware of how your time can be expanded. Seek ways to link the two, beginning with the energies and circumstances each moment offers.

10. *Accept the present as the only time you know you have.* The past is over, and you have its residue for your present. You have the lessons, the accomplishments, the friends and enemies, loved ones and strangers as ties or anchors. These are what you have right now. Tomorrow will be different, partly because it will be different time, partly because of what you will change today. Ultimately the present is all you have to work with—to do what you dream of doing and to become who you want to be.

INDEX

Achievement, 37;
   depression and, 114–115
Activity: depression
   handled by, 120–121;
   reaction to anxiety, 109;
   source of joy, 35
Acute depression, 113–115
Aerobic exercises, 157
Aggression, control of, 17,
   19
Agitation, fear and, 45
Alarm reaction, 134
Alcohol abuse, 123
Alienation, 38
Altruism, 154
Ambiguity, trust and, 69
Anger, 4–5, 11–32
   aggression controlled by,
17, 19; awareness of,
21–22; communications
tool, 15, 17; constructive
use of, 14–19; diary,
19–20; expressing, 16;
handling in others, 30–
32; interpersonal, 25,
27, 29–30; misdirected
energy, 14–15; negative
results of, 13–14;
objective, 25–29;
overreaction, 14;
physical effects of, 18;
profile, 26–27;
reinforcement, 24;
relaxation to control, 25;
self-esteem, threats to,
as producing, 22–23;

NOTES